How to Win
a Local Election

How to Win a Local Election

A COMPLETE STEP-BY-STEP GUIDE

Third Edition

JUDGE LAWRENCE GREY

M. Evans

Lanham • New York • Boulder • Toronto • Plymouth, UK

Published by M. Evans
An imprint of The Rowman & Littlefield Publishing Group, Inc.
4501 Forbes Boulevard, Suite 200, Lanham, Maryland 20706

Estover Road, Plymouth PL6 7PY, United Kingdom

Distributed by NATIONAL BOOK NETWORK

Library of Congress Cataloging-in-Publication Data

Grey, Lawrence.
  How to win a local election : a complete step-by-step guide/ Lawrence Grey.
-- 3rd ed.
    p. cm.
  Includes index.
  ISBN-13: 978-1-59077-131-0 (pbk. : alk. paper)
  ISBN-10: 1-59077-131-1 (pbk. : alk. paper)
  1. Local elections—United States—Handbooks, manuals, etc. 2. Campaign
management—United States—Handbooks, manuals, etc. 3. Political campaigns—
United States—Handbooks, manuals, etc. I. Title.
  JS395.G74 2007
  324.70973—dc22
                                            2007011662

∞™ The paper used in this publication meets the minimum requirements of
American National Standard for Information Sciences—Permanence of Paper for
Printed Library Materials, ANSI/NISO Z39.48-1992.
Manufactured in the United States of America.

For Cathy

MICHAEL P. FRENCH, PHD

Throughout this book I will be telling you to get people, particularly people with special talents, to help you with your campaign. I will also be telling you to make sure that the people that help you know how much you appreciate their help.

In accord with my own advice, I got Dr. Michael P. French to help me with the computer-related parts of this book. He put together the data contained on the disk sold with the book. And he made many of the suggestions about how computers can be used in a campaign.

I appreciate his help, and I want to make sure that people are aware of how much I appreciate it.

— Judge L. Grey

CONTENTS

No man undertakes a trade he has not learned, even the meanest; yet everyone thinks himself sufficiently qualified for the hardest of all trades—that of government.

—Socrates

FOREWORD

The whole process of American democracy starts at the local level. I can't think of any part of the political spectrum of our country that is more important than those elections for county supervisor, school board member, zoning board, mayor, or any of the dozens of other local offices that are voted on each year. These elections can and do affect the average voter as much as or even more than the highly visible campaigns for Congress, the Senate, and even the presidency.

Judge Lawrence Grey has written a thorough handbook for the American man or woman who decides that by running for office he or she can make a difference in the life of the community. *How to Win a Local Election* is a detailed, step-by-step guide that shows the potential candidate the hows and whys of campaigning, from the decision to run to the victory party. There are discussions of campaign themes and strategies, financing, finding and training campaign volunteers, advertising, yard signs and billboards, and going door to door; the book is not only complete but also very readable.

The book is useful for Republicans, Democrats, and Independents. It points out the pitfalls, it details the hard work involved in running for office, and it recognizes the rewards of service to the community. Its lessons apply not only to the first-time candidate but to anyone who wants to run an efficient, effective, and successful campaign.

—Haley Barbour
Former Chairman, Republican National Committee

FOREWORD

Most people—perhaps fewer people today than in the past—see a public life as one of the highest aspirations anyone can hope to achieve. However, politics and politicians are both admired and reviled at the same time in America. We exult in building them up and rejoice in tearing them down over the smallest transgressions. It makes you wonder sometimes why anyone would want to seek a political career in the first place. Politicians are men and women who have a vision for the future and who are not obsessed with the demands of the present. They have a willingness to consider the future impact of decisions made today, and even a willingness to sacrifice on behalf of that future.

This attitude can be found in any politician at any level of government. They see a problem that they want to work to fix—be it large or small, local or national—and they take on the challenge of correcting that problem, not for them and their family today but to prevent that problem from continuing to affect every family in the community.

Every good politician I have ever met has always been a builder. They strive to unite people in the pursuit of the common good. Good politicians are willing not only to find flaws but to roll up their sleeves and go to work every day to find real solutions to the problems facing us.

Fortunately, most people who enter politics do so for good reasons—regardless of party. They want to solve problems. They want to build, not tear down. They appeal to what

Abraham Lincoln called "the better angels of our nature"—our optimism, our hopes, our solidarity, our sense of community, our sense of compassion. To turn that sense into action is what an election campaign is all about. The next question is, how do you win an election? While there are any number of books about winning elections on the national level, that's not where most people begin their careers in politics. They start out much closer to home, in school board elections, town councils, and county legislatures.

In this book, Judge Lawrence Grey sets forth an excellent guide to winning a local election. Although formulating and expressing one's beliefs is relatively easy, spreading the word about these views is often difficult. Putting on a campaign can be quite daunting. This book takes some of the fear out of running for office by explaining the process in clear steps. At the same time, Judge Grey does not oversimplify things nor make them seem easier than they actually are. Campaigns take a great deal of energy and hard work.

I have been through several local races. I managed two Chicago mayoral campaigns and served as a precinct captain in the 44th Ward Organization in the city of Chicago. I even ran for Congress—I lost in the primary. I wish this book was around back then to help me on some of those campaigns.

In a day where money has too much say in who wins and loses elections, this book offers the average person a chance. *How to Win a Local Election* will give anyone who dreams of building a better future for their community the opportunity to act on that dream.

—David Wilhelm
Former Chairman, Democratic National Committee

INTRODUCTION

The United States is a very democratic society. There are about 537,000 elective offices nationwide. While a great amount of money and effort is spent going after the status jobs like congressman, what happens locally is probably more important to the average voter. The trade deficit, our foreign relations with China, and the Federal Reserve Bank's discount rate are all important, of course, but probably not as important as having your garbage picked up or the zoning laws fairly applied. This book is about how to win those very important local elections.

WHAT DO WE MEAN BY A LOCAL ELECTION?

When we talk about a local election, we are not talking about geography; we are talking about an attitude. We are not talking about selling your soul to raise a lot of money so you can hire spin doctors and media consultants. We are talking about a campaign where you, and your friends and supporters, go out and bring your message directly to the voters. We do not ignore media or direct-mail techniques, of course, but when we speak of a local election we mean a campaign where you, as a person, go out and get people to vote for *you* because they know you and like what you stand for. We are talking about democracy in its purest form.

WHO IS THIS BOOK FOR?

This book is for the person who is interested in the local community and wants to win a local election and serve the public in that office. It is not for someone who wants to run only to promote debate on an issue or to advance some cause. This book is not about losing in a good fight. It is about fighting the good fight and *winning!*

In writing it, we have made a few assumptions. One is that the reader is a first-time candidate for public office. As such, some of this material is quite basic, and readers who have been involved in campaigning before might find parts of it too elementary. However, this book also contains comprehensive information and advice on virtually every aspect of the political process, so even experienced readers will find it helpful.

This is a how-to book. It will tell you how to do the things that will get you elected—the important things like how to get your name on the ballot. We also talk about the apparently trivial matters, like getting a map of the district, yet these minor points are not trivial at all but absolutely critical to a successful race.

To some extent, this is as much of a *must-do* book as it is a how-to book. We are not simply telling you how to do things; we are telling you the things you must do to win. Winning is not, as Vince Lombardi said, the only thing, but there is no sense in making a run for elective office unless you are intent on winning. Keep in mind that this book is really nothing more than a lot of good advice. Good advice that is not followed, however, is like good intentions, and as my mother used to say, "The road to Hell is paved with good intentions."

There is such a wide variety of offices, different geographical areas, separate election laws for each state, and peculiar local conditions, so not everything we say will apply to your election. If, as you read this book, you see that the topic we are discussing will apply in your local race, pay attention to what we suggest. We are not merely suggesting that you try it; we are saying that you probably must do it to win the election.

WARNING!

You Cannot Rely Only on What We Say Here!

Occasionally you will see this warning in the book. When you see it, pay particular attention to our comments about checking the local requirements. Each state has its own elections and campaign ethics laws, and these laws fill a book of over a thousand pages, so they cannot be listed here. Even if we could list every requirement for every state and locality, these laws are continually changing and what we say would be out of date by the time this book is published. When you see this warning, it is because our research has shown that first-time candidates often have problems in the area we are discussing, so always make sure to check the local regulations as they apply in your election.   ⇽

LOCAL ISSUES CAMPAIGNS

"All politics is local," said Tip O'Neill, former speaker of the House. We have written this book using the candidate as the focus of our discussion, but there are many local campaigns involving issues, such as township zoning or a local tax levy for the library. If you are interested in a local issue rather than an office, you will still find most of what we say helpful in organizing and winning the election. The only difference between a candidate race and an issue race is that in one you are trying to sell a person and the other you are trying to sell an idea. The mechanics of reaching out to the voters is much the same.

We have decided, as a matter of editorial choice, to write this book in terms of a candidate's election to make it more readable and to avoid clutter. It would be very distracting to the reader to keep flopping back and forth between candidate elections and issues elections, particularly so when most of what we have to say is true for both kinds of races.

For example, when we talk about getting a map of the district or organizing volunteers, the work to be done is virtually identical, so there is no need to discuss an issues campaign separately. Where there is a need to mention issues campaigns separately, we will talk about the differences. For example, candidates must file financial reporting statements. Political committees formed to promote an issue on the ballot must also file in many states, but the reporting requirements are sometimes different.

We will occasionally comment on those differences as they specifically relate to a local issue election campaign, but just about everything we say here about how to win a candidate's race will apply to an issues campaign, too.

STORIES

To illustrate the points I want to make and to keep the book interesting to the reader, I will occasionally tell a story to demonstrate a point. A lot of these stories will be about mistakes, and the author frankly concedes that I regard myself somewhat qualified to write this book because, as the boast goes, "I've done it all." In doing it all, I have been very successful but also have made almost all the mistakes a candidate might make. I have learned from my mistakes and wish to share them so you can avoid the same pitfalls and capitalize on the same successes.

THE OLD HAND

Throughout this book we will suggest that you talk to an "old hand," some veteran of the local political wars. This is one of the best ways to learn about any institution. If you want to know how hospitals really work, for example, a nurse with twenty-five years' experience on the floor would be a better source than a staff physician or a hospital administrator. A sergeant knows more than a general about some things. In politics, it is the same way.

You can learn an awful lot from some old hand who has experience in campaigns in your local area. An old hand can help you avoid mistakes and give you insights into how things really work. Like most of the advice in this book, we have done for ourselves what we suggest you do. We have always had the help of an old hand in our races, and we had one help in writing this book.

Our old hand was Anne Mary "Nancy" Watson, who has been involved in political campaigns all her life. Over the last thirty years, she, too, has done it all, from being a paid professional staff member on congressional and senatorial campaigns to being an advisor and volunteer in local races. Virtually every chapter in this book was given to her for review and comments, and invariably she added suggestions to make this book more helpful, more practical, and more useful to a person planning to win an election.

We appreciate Mrs. Watson's assistance. One of the things she strongly recommends is that we emphasize the need to thank people who help out in your campaign. With her suggestion in mind, we want to thank her for all her help in making this book much more useful to the reader.

⇢ PART I ⇠

PLANNING AND ORGANIZING THE CAMPAIGN

This book is divided into three main parts and has a section of appendixes. We used this format, the three divisions, because it reflects the outline of what should be done, step by step, in a typical campaign. The three parts are:

    I. Planning—Chapters 1 through 9
    II. People—Chapters 10 through 16
    III. Procedures—Chapters 17 through 24

The first part, Planning, talks about all the things you have to do to prepare to run, such as studying your district and learning as much as you can about local conditions. It is the research and organizational part, the thinking part, of a good campaign.

The second part, People, talks about the people in the campaign—everyone from the candidate to the campaign volunteer. To win, you need people to help you, and this part of the book tells how to use those people most efficiently.

The third part of the book, Procedures, discusses the different techniques that are used to reach the voters and how each one can be used most effectively. We discuss the conventional wisdom about each technique and how it is used but also give an admittedly subjective evaluation of each and how effective we think it is.

⇢ 1 ⇠

We have tried to follow a chronology similar to a typical campaign, but that is not always possible. For example, we talk about literature and the campaign brochure in Chapter 17, fund-raising in Chapter 15, and a campaign theme in Chapter 7. All three are closely interrelated because before you can print a brochure, you have to know what it will cost and where the money will come from. We suggest that you read the entire book first, then refer to it as each stage of the campaign develops.

The appendix disk is designed to include useful information that will assist you in your race. We have already mentioned how important it is to check your local election laws, so on the disk we have a list of the addresses and websites of the elections directors for each state where you can get a copy of the regulations and the reporting forms. You can also click on the state code button and get a copy of your state's statutes. The appendixes also contain sample campaign forms that can, after being modified to suit your race, be used to organize and streamline your campaign.

The whole idea of this book is to present a complete campaign strategy that encompasses everything that has to be done in a successful campaign. The format of the book, however, is to break this monumental task down into workable segments that can be achieved one by one. There are chapters on the various things to be done and on the people to do them. We strongly suggest that you have your campaign volunteers read that part of the book that relates to their work. The campaign manager should read Chapter 12, "The Campaign Manager," and the person in charge of mailing should read the chapter on mailing, and so on.

Unless this is a library copy, we suggest that you make notes to yourself in the margins. We make a lot of suggestions, and it may help if you make a note to do the things we suggest.

What we have tried to do here is to write not only a how-to book but a what-to, who-to, when-to, and even a why-to book. Nothing is certain in politics, and this book will not guarantee that you will win, but if you follow what it says and do as we suggest, we can guarantee that you will run an efficient and effective campaign.

THE OFFICE
YOU WANT TO RUN FOR

When a man assumes a public trust, he should consider himself public property.

—Thomas Jefferson

S omebody once asked Abraham Lincoln what the office of president was really like. Lincoln said the question reminded him of the story about a man who was being run out of town on a rail. He was asked what he thought of that, and looked down from the rail and said, "Well, if it weren't for the honor of the thing, I'd rather walk."

This is still a pretty fair description of what it is like to hold elective office. There is a certain amount of honor in being chosen by your fellow citizens to manage the public's affairs, but there is also that element of subjecting yourself to the howling throng.

We are going to presume that you have already considered the drawbacks, but still think that you can contribute to your community, that you can make a difference, that you can handle the public's affairs and do a good job of it. We are also going to presume that you have some idea of which elective office you want to run for.

The first question you have to ask of yourself is the very question that is asked about any candidate: "Is this guy qualified?"

You have to ask that question of yourself because every voter is going to ask it about you. During your campaign, somebody will ask you straight out why you think you are qualified for the job. You have to be ready with a good answer, and to be ready you have to have thought about your answer, about your qualifications. There are official qualifications but also what we call unofficial qualifications.

The official qualifications are usually pretty simple. In this democratic country that encourages public participation in government, it is not hard to meet the official qualifications for most local offices. The official qualifications may vary from state to state and from office to office but generally are the same throughout most of the United States. Basically, all that is required is that you be a registered voter and a resident of the district in which you are running.

We use the words "generally" and "basically" for an important reason. We want to emphasize that the things we talk about here are things in general.

WARNING!

You Cannot Rely Only on What We Say Here!

It is not that what we say is inaccurate but rather that what we say here may not be completely accurate for your state. Not only does each state have its own peculiar election laws, many times the courts in each have interpreted similar election laws quite differently. Local candidates, particularly newcomers, often run afoul of the election laws or the requirements for candidates in their state. One purpose of this book is to help prevent that, but we cannot list all of the state and local election laws.

You must check the local requirements for yourself. You cannot rely on what some person, even some old political hand, tells you. You must check for yourself.

We will repeat this warning over and over again as we discuss the filing requirements, finance reports, and so on, and probably bore you to death with it, but frankly it is one of the best bits of advice you are going to get out of this book.

In talking about the official qualifications, we suggest that you begin with checking out the official requirements for your office. We also suggest that you get into the habit of always checking the local election laws on any question that might come up.

Although, as we said above, the basic qualifications are generally pretty simple, there are many local wrinkles. For example, in one state a teacher may not run for the school board, but in another he may work in one school district but be eligible to run for the school board if he lives in another district. You have to check for any official requirement that may make you unqualified for an office.

There are also special requirements that must be met before you can qualify as a candidate for certain specialized offices. In one state, only a licensed physician can run for coroner, only a certified peace officer can run for sheriff, and only a licensed professional engineer can be a candidate for county engineer. In another state, none of these professional licensures are required. We won't give the names of the states because it really does not matter what the official requirements are in some other state. It only matters what they are in your state, and you have to look that up yourself.

The qualifications are listed in your state code, which is a compilation of the state laws. Many libraries have copies of the state code, and so does every lawyer's office. On the appendix disk we have listed a website entitled "state code" for each state. Using that site, it is fairly easy to find out about the official qualifications. You may be running for an office that is governed by a city charter, or local ordinances, so you have to check that source, but local codes are readily available in libraries and law offices, too.

When you look at the qualifications, also look up the section that deals with the duties of the office—the powers, functions, and areas of responsibility. There may be some duties involved in the job you are not aware of. In public employment, like any employment, it is a good idea to look at the job description before you sign on.

For example, when I was running for county prosecutor I looked up the statutory duties and discovered that in Ohio the prosecutor is given a secret fund from which to make undercover purchases of such things as guns and drugs and that he need not account to anyone for the money. (This law was an open invitation for corruption. One prosecutor, it was rumored, used the money to investigate the source of drugs being sold in his county. Every winter he went to investigate one of the islands in the Caribbean, and to avoid blowing his cover as a tourist, he took his wife along with him. This law has since been changed.) You should know exactly and completely the duties of the office, and the limits of that office, as they are listed in the state code.

There is another reason, kind of a philosophical one, why we suggest you begin by looking up the qualifications and duties in the code. If you do what we tell you to do in this book, there is a very good chance that you are going to win election to office. If you do win, you are going to have to look things up in the code on a regular basis because your office and duties are regulated by law. You ought to begin by learning your way around the state code or city charter. We want to help you to win, but we also want you to be good at the job you're running for. A good official always follows the law, and always checks the code first to see what the law is.

If looking things up in the code or charter seems too intimidating, ask someone in the party or an old hand if they know a friendly lawyer. Lots of lawyers are politically active and would be happy to photocopy the relevant code sections for a good candidate.

Although checking the office out in the state code is not a must-do thing, we strongly recommend it. There are also other, more informal, ways to find out about the job. One of the very best is to attend the meetings of the board or office. If you plan to run for town council or the school board, sit in on the city council or school board meetings and listen to what goes on. Find out what is currently on the agenda and what is likely to come up during the campaign.

Talk to people who have held the job. An incumbent is not likely to give you much help if you are planning to run against him, but if you know someone who has already served in that office, ask him or her about it. Talk to the employees in that office about the work they do and how it might be improved.

Talk to the people who are served by that office or do business with it on a regular basis. If you are running for the housing board, you should ask the head of the tenants union and the president of the landlord association what they expect from a member of the board.

Find out as much as you can about the official duties of that office so that you can think about how you would handle the problems that might come up.

You ought to think about the unofficial qualifications, too. Take the example we used previously—Abraham Lincoln, who is remembered as a great president. He had determination, honesty, courage, a touch of ruthlessness, and the kind of strength this country needed in its darkest hour. None of these are official qualifications for president, and indeed we have had several presidents with few of them, yet the unofficial qualifications are perhaps more important.

These are those personal habits, training, and experience that make you qualified for the job. If you are one of those people who can look at a long column of numbers on a spreadsheet and make sense of it, or who can look at a balance sheet and know almost immediately if the company is making or losing money, you are suited to run for city treasurer. You're the kind of person the rest of us want in that office. If you are a trained CPA, or have ten years' experience handling books, it makes you an even better candidate.

Go for the office you are good at. Some public offices are administrative, where your ability to handle a staff and serve the public is the major criterion. Are you good at managing paperwork? Can you handle subordinates? Others are more legislative, like alderman or councilwoman, where the main function is to listen to competing interests and make policy choices. Are you good at listening to people? Can you make a decision and stick with it?

Do you have the time to do what is involved in the office? Many offices are part time, but with all the meetings, conferences, and consultations, they are quite demanding.

Evaluate yourself. Answer these questions about your personal and professional qualifications.

1. What can I contribute?
2. How could I do the job better?
3. Why do I want to do this?
4. How much time can I give to the campaign?
5. How much time can I give to the job?
6. What will I get from it?
7. What will I have to give up?
8. What does my family think?
9. Will I be hurt and angry at rejection?

We would also suggest that in making a personal inventory you might want to think about getting a physical checkup before you decide to run for office. Campaigning is often a grueling, exhausting effort. President Clinton talked himself hoarse in the last days of his campaign in 1992 and had to cut back on speeches in 1996. Poor Bob Dole looked terrible as election day drew near. Tired candidates make mistakes like calling someone a "Macaca" (in the 2006 U.S. Senate race in Virginia). Of course they were out there campaigning every day, but the only real difference between your race and theirs is that in a local contest, the distance between campaign stops is shorter. You will be working every day, too. And it is hard work to boot!

When you have done this personal inventory, and found out all you can about the duties of the office, and learned about all the official and unofficial qualifications, then ask yourself: Would I vote for me? If the answer is yes, then you must have some reason why. Get those reasons straight in your head. It is the first step in your campaign, but you will get that question over and over as you campaign. If you know what you're after, and know why you can do the job, it will come across to the voters.   ✦

Having picked your office, now let's get on to the other chapters and see about how you can win it.

2

ELECTION STATISTICS

Not everything that can be counted counts, and not everything that counts can be counted.

—Albert Einstein

The last event in an election is when they count the votes. Oddly enough, counting the votes is one of the first steps in your campaign. To win, you have to ask yourself: How many votes do I need, and where will I get them?

You have to begin by picking the number. You have to decide how many votes it will take, probably, to give you a victory. That number is likely to be a lot smaller than you might think at first.

In analyzing election statistics there are two cardinal principles. One is that many Americans don't vote. The other is that you don't need all the votes, or even most of the votes. You need only 50 percent of the votes, plus one. With these two principles in mind, you have to get the election results in your race for at least the last four elections and decide how many votes it takes to win your race.

Let's try an example. A woman who had been a law clerk for our court wanted to run for city law director in the small city where she lived. It had a population of about 35,000. Of that 35,000, only about 64 percent of the population was registered to vote, so there were only about 22,400 voters.

This is where the propensity of Americans to not vote comes in. Although there were over 22,000 registered voters in the city, municipal elections were held in off years, that is, in years when there were no other major races. When there is a big, statewide race, like for governor or senator, there tends to be a bigger voter turnout. Some people vote only when there is a presidential race, so in those years there is a substantially larger number of people going to the polls. Although who gets elected mayor probably has more effect on the average person's life than who gets elected president, in local elections there is a falloff in voter interest. Some voters will mark their ballots for the big races at the head of the ballot and not vote in the smaller local elections on the ballot. This is called voter fatigue.

In checking the election statistics for the last four races for law director in this small city, we found that only about 30 percent actually voted in the law director's race. The total number of votes cast on both sides for the office of law director was about 6,600 on the average. To win such a race, then, the candidate needs 50 percent, about 3,300, plus one more vote to get a majority.

The first thing to do is to take care of that "plus one vote." Ask your mother if she will vote for you. We do not suggest you ask your spouse. In one famous case, a candidate got only one vote—his own. His wife was quoted in the newspaper as saying she didn't think he had a chance so she didn't vote for him. The newspaper gleefully reported this under a headline that read, "One man, one vote!" Politics is a tough business.

When you get your mother's assurance that she will vote for you, then start thinking about the number, the other 50 percent. This number is the focus of your campaign.

Just thinking about running for an office can be intimidating. The law clerk was daunted by the idea of running in a city of 35,000 people, but when a review of the election statistics showed that she really was after only 10 percent of that number, she had a much better perspective on what she had to do.

Thirty-three hundred voters, and perhaps her mother, was an attainable goal for her.

Very early on in your campaign, you have to pick your target number. You have to target an exact number of how many votes you will have to get in order to win. You determine that number by looking at the results in past elections and by analyzing board of elections statistics.

All elections boards keep records of the results in every election going back for several years. These records are public records and can be obtained at your local elections office. The people who work in elections offices are usually pretty good about helping you find what you need. We have always found them to be polite and helpful.

You should keep in mind, however, that elections offices are always in a boom-or-bust cycle. Shortly before the filing deadline for the primary they are very busy, so if you go in then and ask to see the statistics, they might give you short shrift. A week later, they will probably have plenty of time and be glad to help. The best time is long before the filing deadline, not so much because it is easier for the elections office clerks but because the earlier you pick your number, the sooner you will know what you have to do to win. You can often find the election statistics by going to the website of the state elections officer, but not always. In some states the results of statewide elections are kept in the main office, while local statistics are kept locally. But those local results are usually available through the Internet also.

Analyzing the statistics is fairly simple. You look to see how other races turned out, paying particular attention to those years where there was a race similar to yours. A three-way race is a lot different than a one-on-one contest, and of course the winning number is lower. If one year there was a hot local issue, like a tax levy, it was likely to have increased voter turnout for that year, and you have to take that into account.

Sometimes, it is hard to tell exactly. Your opponent may be an incumbent who has not had any opposition in the last couple of times out. If that's the case, you can look at comparable races in other nearby districts. For example, see how many votes it took to get elected alderman in the adjoining wards when the race was contested.

Try to estimate the falloff rate, the voter fatigue factor, in your race. State and national races increase voter turnout, but these part-time voters don't vote in all the races on the ballot. For example, our sample city has 22,400 voters, but only 14,700 of them voted for president in 1988. There was also a race for the state supreme court justice on the ballot, but only about 10,000 of them voted in the supreme court race. So although there were actually 14,700 people who went into the voting booth, 4,700 of them, 32 percent, did not think the supreme court race was important enough to bother voting.

If you are in an "unimportant" race, sometimes called a low-profile race, there will be this falloff in voter interest, and you have to know approximately how big it will be. (We will talk about getting some votes from these falloff voters later.)

The election statistics will tell you the results in the last four or five elections, the total number who voted, the number who voted in your race, and the number who voted in similar races. With this information, you come up with an average number of people who are likely to vote in your race. Divide that by two, and you have your target number.

Once you have picked your number, you have to sit down with your campaign people and decide how you are going to get that number, precinct by precinct. If the people in Ward 3 Precinct C are madder than hell about the sewers backing up, you can look to getting some votes there. If, on the other hand, they just had a testimonial dinner for the councilman at the new recreation center he had built in the ward, and five hundred people showed up, you can forget about winning there.

Try to locate the swing precincts, that is, the precincts with swing voters. Few people are voting a straight ticket nowadays, but party affiliation still counts to some extent. Even many who call themselves Independents still tend, all things being equal, to vote more for candidates of one party than another. A swing voter can be defined as one who votes for the particular candidate but usually not on the basis of party affiliation.

In order to identify the swing precincts, look at several election results with very lopsided margins. If you see a precinct where the Republican candidate garnered a very small percentage of the vote, it is safe to assume that this number represents the base, hard-core Republican vote in that precinct. Any Republican candidate can expect to get that many votes. Do the same in a few races involving Democratic losers, and this will establish the base Democratic vote. Compare these base votes with the total votes cast, and you will have an idea about the precincts in your district.

Table 2.1 shows the results from one ward in one election. Just by looking at them you can get a good idea of how the voters who live there vote.

Table 2.1 Sample Election Results

	Republican Vote	*Democratic Vote*
Governor	1,017 (56%)	804 (44%)
Attorney General	774 (42%)	1,050 (58%)
Secretary of State	1,045 (57%)	777 (43%)
State Treasurer	1,079 (61%)	689 (39%)
State Representative	563 (30%)	1,319 (70%)
County Auditor	1,107 (58%)	789 (42%)
County Commissioner	965 (50.5%)	896 (49.5%)
Sheriff	1,287 (72%)	501 (28%)

The Republicans won six of eight races, and the most typical margin was over 55 percent. The Democratic attorney general, however, seems to be a popular vote getter. The Democratic state representative got substantially more votes than anyone else. This state representative appears hard to beat, so the Republicans probably put up some sacrificial lamb to run against him. Nonetheless, that candidate got 563 votes, which indicates a core Republican strength of about 500-plus votes, no matter who the candidate is.

The Republican sheriff was the second highest vote getter, and his race demonstrates the hard-core Democratic vote is about 500 also.

Look at the commissioner's race. Almost all the other Republicans got over 1,000 votes, but in the commissioner's race the Democrat cut into the typical Republican margin and, by reaching the swing voters, came close to winning.

From this very simple set of statistics you learned a lot about this one ward. About 1,800 will vote. Five hundred will vote Democrat and 500-plus will vote Republican, leaving 800 swing voters who tend to favor the Republican candidates. As the commissioner's race shows, these swing voters can be reached by a Democrat with a good campaign. Every swing vote counts for two, because it is not just plus one for you but also minus one for your opponent. This is the kind of information the election statistics give you.

With this information, you can determine which precincts:

1. Are favorable to candidates from your party regardless of the individual candidate's strength.
2. Are unfavorable to candidates from your party.
3. Contain the swing voters.
4. Have an issue that motivates the voters.

You can build on the base of voters who identify with you because of your party affiliation, but you cannot presume on them. You will have to campaign to these people, but elections are won and lost by reaching the swing voters, the people whose votes are up for grabs. A successful candidate must take his campaign to these swing voters. Once you have determined what your base vote will be, you can see how many swing voters you will need to win. The statistics will tell you where they are.

You have to go through the election statistics, precinct by precinct, and think to yourself, "I can get so many votes in this precinct, but not so many in that one, and I will lose by a lot of votes in the other one," and so forth. When you have done your precinct-by-precinct analysis, you will have a much better idea of how you can get that magic number of votes.

When you analyze the election statistics, you will know from the beginning how the election is likely to turn out

1. if you do nothing, or
2. if you work like a dog.

You will see that you can count on getting 350 votes in good old Democratic Ward 5 Precinct C easily. You will also realize that you will have to work very hard even to get 150 votes in Republican Ward 5 Precinct A. So if you are going to win at all, you have to get at least 250 votes from the voters in swing Ward 5 Precinct B.

By using this kind of analysis, you will already have begun to focus your campaign efforts even though you have not even filed yet. The whole purpose of reviewing the election statistics is to break down an overwhelming task into smaller workable units. It gives you a real advantage to know at the very beginning that you can win if you get 250 votes in Precinct 5B. (We will talk later in this book about finding a precinct volunteer in 5B to help you win there.)

One main purpose in analyzing the statistics is so you will not be intimidated by trying to go after 35,000 people, or 22,000 voters, or even 3,500 voters. Having a workable, attainable target number for each precinct gives a candidate a tremendous psychological edge.

When looking for that magic number, however, one thing may occur to you. Your opponent may be unbeatable. There are many competent, popular, and experienced officeholders who know how to win elections. Your analysis may show that you probably cannot win. This, too, is worth knowing because you don't want to get into a race you can't win. If the votes aren't there, they aren't there. If you have to rely on the "heart attack strategy," where your only chance of winning depends on your opponent dying of a heart attack, then perhaps you should not file petitions.

There are, on the other hand, many jerks in public office who can be easily picked off by a competent campaign. If your opponent is one who can be picked off, it will show in the election statistics. They will show exactly where and how you can do it. If there is an open seat with no incumbent, and you're looking for an edge, the election statistics will show where it can be found.

Reviewing election statistics is a subjective kind of analysis, of course, and whether you can win or not is often a very iffy question. Realistically, your analysis is most likely to indicate that you might have a chance of winning, might be able to reach that magic number, if everything goes right. It won't, but even at that, if your analysis leads you to conclude that you might win, then we think you should go for it. As the old cowboy said, "There was never a horse that couldn't be rode, there was never a rider that couldn't be throwed."

The election statistics will tell you what it takes to win, what the target number is, and where those votes are.

3

LOCAL ELECTION LAWS: GETTING ON THE BALLOT

He is half done who has already begun.

—Horace

In April 1992, there was an article on the op-ed page of the New York Times written by Larry Rockefeller, who wanted to run in the Republican primary for U. S. senator and had circulated nominating petitions. He complained bitterly in the article that when he filed his petitions with the board of elections they used every petty defect in form to invalidate the petition. If they found one bad signature, instead of not counting it, they threw out the whole petition and all the good names with it. As a result of this hanky-panky, Rockefeller did not get on the ballot.

Larry Rockefeller is a scion of one of the best-known political families in America and a man with sufficient resources to challenge any shenanigans in court, and still they did a job on him and on his nominating petitions. The saddest part is that it was all legal. Think about that. If they can do it to him, the same thing can happen to you.

While there are as many variations as there are states, getting on the ballot is ordinarily done by nominating petition. A person seeking to run for an office goes to the elections office and obtains the petition forms for that office. He fills out the petition form as candidate and signs it. In some states, the candidate's signature must be notarized. In some states the nomination form is called a "declaration of candidacy" and in other states you must file both a declaration of candidacy and nominating petitions.

Underneath the candidate's part of the form there are lines for people, who must be registered voters, to sign their names petitioning that the candidate's name be put on the ballot. The candidate obtains the signatures of the required number of voters on his petitions and files them with the elections office. The board checks the petition to see if the names are valid and if the petitions contain the required number of signatures. If so, they certify the petition, and the candidate's name is put on the ballot. This is how it is done, in theory. In practice, it is often quite another matter.

Warning!
You Cannot Rely Only on What We Say Here!

In doing your nominating petitions you must strictly comply with your state's requirements. You must learn what the local requirements are. We can give examples of the law in some states, but we cannot tell you what is the law in your own state. We can tell you, though, that you must do it right or you won't get on the ballot. ↞

PRIMARY AND GENERAL ELECTIONS

There are basically two kinds of elections, the primary and the general, and usually the candidate files petitions to get on the ballot in the primary election. The primary ballot contains the names of all the candidates from one party who want to run for that office. Whoever wins the primary election will be on the ballot as the party's candidate in the general election. The general election decides who will hold that office.

In some elections, there is no primary, but nominating petitions are still used. The candidate circulates and files petitions. If he has the minimum number of signatures, his name is put on the ballot in the general election along with all other candidates who file valid petitions.

In another variation, the party candidates file petitions and run in the primary, but a nonparty candidate may file petitions for that office as an independent. The two winners of the primaries, plus the independent candidate, will be on the ballot in the general election, the so-called three-way race. Some states use a party convention to select primary candidates, but other party candidates can get on the ballot by petition. Some states use the convention nomination system for some offices and petitions for others.

In still other elections, called "bedsheet ballot elections," all candidates file petitions for one seat out of several and the top vote getters win. For example, there may be three seats open on the board of commissioners and eight candidates who file petitions for commissioner. All eight names are on the ballot, and the voters can vote for any three names. The top three vote getters win.

On the other hand, the three commissioner seats may be elected separately. Each commissioner seat is distinguished, usually by the date the term begins (e.g., commissioner, term beginning January 1; commissioner, term beginning January 2). In that case, the nominating petition has to state specifically which term the candidate is running for.

We could go on and on like this, but there is not much use in telling you about all the variations in local election laws. It does not matter unless you are working for a PhD in political science. It is the law in your area that counts, and you have to check that out yourself. Your nominating petitions have to comply with local law, no matter what.

The nominating petition system is, unfortunately, subject to a lot of abuse. Reasonable regulations are adopted to promote democracy and foster efficient elections. It is not unreasonable, for example, to require that a candidate get some voters' names on his petition. After all, if he can't get a few signatures, he is not likely to get any votes and it is a waste of taxpayers' money to have his name on the ballot.

Too often, however, a reasonable regulation is subverted for political purposes. The "Ins" use the law to keep the "Outs" out. In one state, a Democrat or a Republican can get on the ballot with 50 signatures on the nominating petition, but a third-party candidate or an Independent needs 250. To get on the ballot for Judge of the Civil Court of Bronx County, New York, one must obtain signatures from 1 percent of the registered voters, but that means a Republican needs about 1,500 while a Democrat has to have about 4,000 names.

Even when some of these roadblocks have been removed, the Ins have resorted to hypertechnical applications of the law to disqualify candidate petitions. In one case, the candidate had fifty names, just exactly the minimum number of signatures required, but state law allowed a signer to withdraw his name from a petition even after it had been filed. The opposition got one of the signers to withdraw his name (I'm sure he was well paid), and the candidate's petitions were declared invalid because he had only forty-nine names, one short. In another case, a woman had just married the candidate and moved in with him. She filled out a new voter registration card and signed his petition using her married name and new address. At the elections office, they held up the filing of her new registration card, invalidated her signature on the petition on the grounds that she was not listed as a voter, and then filed the card. That's the kind of stuff that goes on.

This is not to say that this sort of thing goes on everywhere. The state of Kentucky, admirably, has done away with this kind of nonsense by simply requiring only two or four valid signatures for many local offices. Kentucky is the exception, and states like California, New York, and Ohio (and probably your state) are the rule. The rule is: Even if you try to comply with the petition requirements, they will use hypertechnical interpretations to try to invalidate your petitions.

In order to avoid this, the people who circulate your nominating petitions have to be carefully instructed on what to do and what not to do. We will discuss the instructions later, but first we want to list some of the common problems that come up on nominating petitions, so that you can have some idea of what the instructions ought to include.

First of all, the candidate's portion of the nominating petition must be completed accurately. If the candidate's portion of the petition is not correct, the entire petition will be declared invalid regardless of the number of valid signatures on it. For example, if the petition form requires the candidate's home address and precinct of residence, that must be included. If the candidate's signature is required to be notarized, then it must be notarized, and so on.

Keep in mind that although we use the phrase "nominating petition," the petition itself is often composed of several sheets. The petition form may have spaces for ten to twenty-five signatures, so if you need fifty or one hundred names, you will have to use separate sheets. Each separate sheet is called a part petition. Each part petition must be valid by itself (i.e., comply with all regulations).

Once the petition has the candidate's part properly filled out, it is given to a circulator who gets people to sign it. Sometimes the candidate can be a circulator, but not everyone can be a circulator. Most local laws have specific requirements for the person who circulates the petition, even if it is the candidate himself.

On most petitions, there is a part for the circulator to fill out, also. For example, after the circulator gets the signatures, he must certify at the end of the petition the number of signatures and that he witnessed each person sign. Sometimes this certification must also be notarized. If the circulator's portion is incorrect, none of the signatures on that part petition will be valid. Always check the requirements for circulators.

Even if the candidate's and the circulator's certifications are proper, some of the individual signatures might be declared invalid. Many of the petition forms we have looked at have a space after the signer's address for the person's resident precinct. This is to help the elections people when they check because they keep the lists of registered voters' names by precinct. In some areas, each part petition can only contain signatures from one precinct to make validation of the names easier. In light of the fact that many elections offices are now fully computerized and names can be checked without reference to the voting precinct, these requirements are archaic, but they are still on the books and still used to trap the unwary. Be sure to check if your state makes having the precinct mandatory, or whatever, because the signature will not be valid without it.

Not everyone can sign a petition. Generally, the signer must be a registered voter, and usually must be of the same political party as the candidate, and only Independents can sign Independent candidates' petitions. In some states, however, anybody can sign, regardless of party affiliation. The signer almost always has to be a resident of that voting district (i.e., live in the same ward, town, county, etc.) that the candidate is running in.

Illegible signatures are often not counted, not because of any nefarious politicking but simply because the signature cannot be read. Ask the signers to write clearly.

There is no end to the things that can invalidate a signature or a petition, so the best bet is to get more names on the petition than you actually need. The general rule of thumb is 3 to 1. If you need one hundred valid names, file petitions containing three hundred names. But even that can get you into trouble, because most states have a maximum number of names a candidate can submit. The validators at the board of elections do not have the time to search through a petition with one hundred signatures to just find one or two valid names, so limiting the names or part petitions to be filed makes sense.

This, too, is a reasonable restriction that is subverted when carried to extremes. You would think that if a candidate filed more than the maximum, they could just look at the maximum number and not look at the extra names. Instead, they invalidate the entire petition, so the rule of thumb of 3 to 1 becomes 2.9 to 1, to avoid that trap.

Nominating petitions and the many pitfalls they entail is one area where talking to an old hand can be useful. We have a whole chapter about having a person who knows the ropes advising you in your race. Read the chapter on the old hand, and talk to an experienced person about your petitions before you even begin to circulate them. He or she can tell you what to watch out for in your local area.

When you do begin to circulate your petitions, don't just give the circulator the part petition. Include an instruction sheet for the circulators that tells them exactly what to do to ensure the signatures will be properly validated. Your instruction sheet might look something like the example on the following page.

All petitions have to be filed by a certain date before the election, which may be weeks or even months before the actual election day. Check your local filing date deadline. Late petitions are not accepted in any state.

After you get the petitions out to the circulators, you have to get them back on time. "On time" means with enough time before the filing deadline for you to go over them carefully. You should check your own petitions with the same nitpicking zeal that the elections office will use. If you find a mistake, it can be corrected. If they find a mistake, you are out.

When you start getting the petitions back, you may find you have more than enough names for the three-to-one rule. However, you may find that you have only near the minimum number, or that there is a problem with one of your part petitions. If one of your petitions is invalidated, you may not get on the ballot. It is better to throw out the problem part petition and get more names on a new one, which you know is done correctly. In order to be able to do this, of course, means that you have to plan to get the petitions out, signed, and back and still leave yourself time enough to check and get even more names if you need them.

Speaking of time and more names, we are going to mention a campaign strategy here. We will talk about campaign strategy in detail in other parts of the book, but we want to mention this strategy because it relates to petition signing. If you have plenty of time, you may want to get far more petition signatures than you actually need. In one city councilman race, the minimum number was twenty-five and the maximum was seventy-five names.

INSTRUCTIONS TO PETITION CIRCULATORS
***Only Registered Democrats Who Live in Water Township
May Circulate This Petition!***

1. Only registered voters may sign. If people are not sure if they are registered, do not have them sign.
2. The person must sign his or her name and address in ink, and be sure to ask the signer to write legibly because illegible signatures will be invalidated. Have a clipboard or other hard surface for them to write on.
3. Have the precinct map with you.
4. Only voters from one precinct may sign your petition. Signers from other precincts will not be counted.
5. The signature of the voter must be followed by the voter's precinct of residence. Most signers will not know their precinct, so have the map, and be ready to tell them what precinct they live in.
6. Do not complete the circulator's affidavit yourself. Bring it to headquarters, or call Jane at 555-2938, so we can check it for accuracy before you certify it.
7. The filing deadline is March 27th, so all petitions must be back no later than March 21st.

Thanks for your help with this.

The candidate actually went out and got 627 names. He used petition signing as a chance to campaign, to talk to the voters in his ward, months before the election. He filed petitions with only seventy names, of course, but he used the other names on his petitions as the database for his campaigning.

He sent thank you notes to every signer right after the filing deadline, and as election drew closer, he asked if they would volunteer, contribute, or put up a yard sign. This was very effective. The people who signed his petition were very likely to vote for him, and out of about 2,500 likely voters in the ward, he had signed up 627 (25 percent) in advance. Remember what we said about the winning number being 50 percent plus one.

There is one final point that should be made about nominating petitions and the need for accuracy. Not only do your petitions have to be accurate, but your opponent's petitions also have to comply with the law exactly, as the following story demonstrates.

I have complained that hypertechnical applications of the election laws are unreasonable and unfair, so the story that follows is, I admit, a bit hypercritical.

In 1988, I was running for reelection as judge and did not expect any real opposition. I had hoped to get a free ride and run unopposed, but just before the deadline another candidate filed petitions. When someone files in against you, no matter who it is, you have to work hard. You don't get elected by assuming you are going to win; you get elected by assuming the other guy can beat you. There are only two ways to run— unopposed and scared.

This other candidate was a weak opponent. He had filed petitions for municipal judge in 1987 but was thrown off the ballot because he put the wrong date on his petitions. I did not think he would make the same mistake twice, but I checked. Incredible! He did it again. He had the wrong date, and this was brought to the attention of the board of elections, which threw him off the ballot. He sued and took the case all the way to the Ohio Supreme Court, but to no avail.

Always check your opponent's nominating petitions and protest any noncompliance. If you can get him off the ballot and run unopposed, this is always easier, cheaper, and much less exhausting for you as a candidate. I do not agree, for very good public policy reasons, with the way some of the election laws in Ohio are interpreted, but when push came to shove, I took advantage of them. He was off the ballot and I was unopposed. Instead of working like a dog all summer long in 1988, I had the time to take the family to Yellowstone and watch Old Faithful while my opponent's political ambitions went up in smoke.

Do your nominating petitions right, because there will always be somebody to make sure you do, or keep you off the ballot if you don't.

4

FINANCIAL REPORTING

In foreign countries it is called corruption. In
Washington it is called lobbying.

> —Anonymous

Money doesn't talk, it swears.

> —Bob Dylan

There is no question about the importance of money in a campaign, and we will talk more about fund-raising and such later in this book, but for now we want to talk about the financial reporting requirements. Basically these laws are do-gooder legislation, an attempt by social scientists to eliminate the political advantage people with money have over the people without money. Living as we do in a capitalist society, these laws are not likely to have the desired effect. The simple fact is that people with money always have the advantage—in food, housing, education, health care, but above all in politics.

Even the ivory tower theorists realize this is the way life is, but they believe that if the public knows who is contributing to a candidate's election or knows where his money is coming from, the voters will have a better chance of evaluating the candidate and his or her positions.

There is some validity in this. It is not so much that a candidate will sell his soul to get contributions but rather that political money tends to seek out the candidates. The National Rifle Association (NRA), for example, will not try to get a candidate to adopt a strong right to bear arms position. Instead, it will look to the candidates who own guns, or hunt, or trap shoot and already think the way the NRA thinks. In a similar vein, the state medical association political action committee (PAC) is not likely to support a lawyer running for the legislature when it knows he has made a successful career winning medical malpractice cases. So to that extent, public reporting of how any candidate is financing his campaign is a relevant issue for the voter to think about.

Because of this, most states have laws which require candidates for public office to file statements disclosing how their campaign is being financed. Campaign financing laws are as varied and as contradictory as the election laws described in an earlier chapter. Each state has different laws and different standards, and even states which have similar laws have different wrinkles. For example, in Tennessee the financial report is not made to the elections office but to the Tennessee Registry of Election Finance. If you have received and spent less than $1,000 you may file a simple form, but over $1,000 requires detailed records. Since Tennessee has primaries in both May and August, plus the general election in November, there are at least half a dozen different filing deadlines.

In California, a candidate must file a statement of intent before soliciting or receiving any contribution or expenditure of any personal funds. If it is expected that there will be less than $1,000, you can use the short form. Both are filed at the office where you first filed as a candidate. When you go over $1,000, you have to file at the same office, but also with the secretary of state, who will assign your campaign an ID number. Arkansas and Vermont both use $500 as the minimum standard for campaign reporting, but in Arkansas, the $500 only covers contributions, while in Vermont, if the candidate accepts contributions or spends in excess of $500, he must file. The Ohio candidate who accepts no contributions is not required to file a financing statement before the election but must file after the election. The Connecticut candidate who accepts no contributions must file before and after the election, but only if he has expended $1,000. The Idaho candidate must report any of his own money that he spends. In New Jersey, you must report to the division of elections "street money," which is passing out cash on election day. You must report this "street money," but it cannot be used to buy votes. Yeah, right! We could go on and on, but to no purpose.

If our comment on financial reporting seems a bit cynical, it is because these laws, like most laws adopted by reformers, tend to go overboard. Although robbers and rapists are entitled to a presumption of innocence, financial reporting laws are premised on the presumption of guilt—that anyone who runs for public office must be either a liar or a thief. While there is no doubt that large amounts of money can affect the outcome of an election, in many small local races there is simply not the kind of money to be so concerned about. In these races, the financial reporting laws are little more than pitfalls for the inexperienced, unwary candidate.

For example, a man I know ran for a local office and paid for a small ad in a newspaper. He dutifully reported the expenditure when he filed his finance statement but did not include the newspaper's street address on the form. He got a computer-generated letter saying the address of all persons to whom expenditures were made had to be listed. Since the newspaper was the largest daily in the state, and since the newspaper office was right across the street from the state office building, he figured it would not be necessary to get new forms and file an amended statement. He just ignored the letter. Three months later he was cited for violation of the reporting laws and fined fifty dollars. This was petty bureaucracy at its worst. (If you get elected, perhaps you can see to it that some bureaucrats get fired for this kind of nonsense.) Still, it made him look bad, and his opponent used it against him in the next election.

While we can make editorial comments about the foolishness of financial reporting in local races where there is so little money involved, the reality for you is that you must comply exactly with the financial reporting requirements in your state. Candidates for almost every office in almost every state have to file some kind of financing statements on official forms. In some states the reports are handled by the elections office, and in other states they are handled by the state ethics office and are called elections reports or ethics reports. For simplicity's sake, we shall refer to them by the general heading of "financial reports." Often these forms are confusing and it is easy to make a mistake, and making a mistake can cost you the election or even be a criminal offense. So what are the requirements in your state?

WARNING!
You Cannot Rely on What We Tell You!

As we said in Chapter 1 and in Chapter 3, these requirements are something you have to find out for yourself. You cannot rely on what you read here. You cannot rely on what someone tells you. You cannot rely on what was done in the past, because the financial reporting laws are often amended. You have to get a copy of the campaign finance reporting law, read it, understand it, and follow it exactly.

Getting a copy of the reporting requirements is not difficult. In most states, when a person presents his nominating petitions for filing, the elections office is required to give him a copy of the election laws, the forms to be filled out, and notification of dates when they have to be filed. We would suggest that you not wait until then. You really should get this information early on in the planning stages of your campaign. Usually the local elections office has booklets and forms for distribution to would-be candidates. If you cannot get this information locally, contact the state elections director. The street address, phone number, and website address of the chief elections officer for each state is listed on the appendix disk. There is also a site for that state's code.

Each elections office website has information about the requirements for financial reporting, but some states are much more candidate friendly than others. The Arkansas elections website has a publication you can download entitled "Plain English Handbook for Candidates," but the Adobe printer said it was 256 pages! That's an awful lot of plain English. In Ohio, you have to hunt through the website trying to find the financial filing requirements for candidates.

Oregon, in contrast, has a very helpful website explaining the duties of the candidate and simple readable forms. It starts with a form entitled "Certificate of Limited Contributions and Expenditures," for smaller campaigns, and then lists others for larger campaigns. Kansas has an excellent site. It has all its forms on its website, and if you are running in Kansas, the simplest thing to do is to download the forms and fill them in as you go. You can do that in any state with good forms for downloading. North Carolina has a campaign treasurer training program and a campaign reporting software which you can download. This seems to me like a great idea if you want accurate and consistent reporting. Several other states are considering such software.

As a candidate, it is your job to know what the financial reporting requirements are and to see to it that they are obeyed, but a candidate should not waste valuable time if it can be done by someone else. It should not be the candidate, and in some states it cannot be the candidate. (Always check these things out.)

Try to name one responsible person to be in charge of all financial reporting matters. It should be someone who pays attention to detail, the kind of person who not only balances his checkbook every month, but when he does, finds that it balances perfectly without any mistakes. You know the type—one who, if there is a discrepancy, thinks the bank made a mistake. Talk to that person and go over the requirements with him or her. Be sure he or she learns exactly what is required, how important the job is, and how much you appreciate not having to worry about this.

Essentially, the finance reporting laws require the candidate to create a paper trail, so that there is some kind of documentation for all contributions and for all expenditures. In creating the paper trail, you maintain documentation on every dime that comes in or goes out, so that when you file the report, you have the records to support it.

One of the best ways to set up a set of books for this information is to begin by looking at the reporting form for your state. If those forms have separate categories for cash contributions, contributions by check, and in-kind contributions, then the best way to keep your records is by using those same categories. Keep a separate list of the names of each cash, check, and in-kind contributor separately. If, as my unfortunate friend discovered, they want the street addresses of every one, then have those street addresses written down so they will be available when you fill out the official form for filing.

If the forms have separate categories for expenditures under $25 but require a receipt for any expenditure over $25, then your campaign books ought to have those separate categories and you must be sure to get those receipts. Using the reporting form format helps to eliminate mistakes because if you follow the forms, you are unlikely to leave out required information.

For a very small campaign, you might make copies of the forms themselves and use them as bookkeeping worksheets, just penciling in the required information as it becomes available. When reporting time comes, you can transfer the data from one form to the other, check it carefully, and file that.

We strongly suggest that you get a checking account for the campaign. Even if you are financing the campaign by yourself and do not expect to get any contributions, a separate checking account is very handy. In some states, a separate account is required. (Check your state's requirements.)

All contributions and all expenditures should go through this account, and only one person (not the candidate) should be able to draw checks on this account. Since one person is handling all contributions and expenditures and is seeing that it is done through one checking account, obviously that person ought to be the one who takes care of preparing and filing the campaign financial report.

He should check on the filing deadlines for the financing reports both for the primary and for the general election. This, too, varies from state to state. Most states require financial reports so many days before the primary and after the primary, and so many days before and after the general election. Also learn where they are to be filed. Some states require that all reports be filed in one location, usually with the state's chief elections officer, such as the secretary of state. In other states, it is done at the same office where you filed your petitions, and in still others candidates for local offices file with the local board of elections while candidates for state offices file with the state elections director. *Always check this out.*

Campaigns get hectic. Things tend to get done at the last minute. We have seen a lot of races where somebody will come rushing in to the board of elections office five minutes before the deadline, and lots where they show up five minutes late and suffer the consequences. Knowing when to file and where to file, and having the information recorded so as to make filling out the form an easy task, simplifies meeting the deadline. If you don't have good records, if you are not sure where to file, there is a better than even chance you will miss a deadline.

We have suggested that you put one person in charge, so get somebody you can rely on. But do not forget that legally it is your individual responsibility to comply with the law. You, the candidate, have to make these deadlines. You might win the primary, and then get a lot of bad press because you filed your financial report late or did it wrong. At best, it makes you look inept. At worst, you might get thrown off the ballot or be charged with violation of the election laws.

The filing deadlines should be prominently posted on the campaign calendar. We will talk more about that calendar in a later chapter, but be sure the deadlines dates are there marked in red.

One final point about reporting. Always look at your opponent's preelection financial report after it is filed. If it is not correct, you may want to issue a news release saying he is a nice enough fellow but just can't seem to do anything right. Even if it is correct, see where he is getting his money; see who is backing him. You may find a good issue to campaign on by a careful review of his financial report. ⤶

5

DISTRICT GEOGRAPHY AND DEMOGRAPHY

Without geography you're nowhere.

—Jimmy Buffett

The first office I ran for was Athens County prosecuting attorney. Athens is a rural county with little villages, hardly more than clusters of houses, in some of the more remote townships. Since these out-of-the-way places tended to be ignored, I figured I could get some votes by going door to door. As I was driving down a gravel township road, I saw this old man sitting in a rocking chair in his front yard close to the road and stopped.

I introduced myself, told him I was running for Athens County prosecutor, and he invited me to sit down and talk for a while. It was a nice day, and as we were talking a small herd of deer came out of the woods to drink at a small pond just across the road. All in all it was a pleasant chat, but as I got up to leave, the old man said, "Well son, I think you'd do a good job, and I wish you luck, but I ain't gonna vote for you." I was a bit taken aback and asked him why not. He pointed down the road and said, "Do you see that spot where the gravel changes color? That's the county line. Hell, boy, you're in Washington County!" That nice old man just wanted someone to talk to, but he taught me an invaluable lesson.

GEOGRAPHY

"Where do I campaign?" is a basic, but important, question. You have to know, precisely, the geographical boundaries of your district because campaigning outside your district is a dead loss.

Most races are not in rural areas but in urban or suburban areas, but knowing where the lines are is just as important. If one side of the street is in precinct A but the other side is in precinct B, which is not in your district, going door to door or passing out literature on the wrong side of the street is just like campaigning outside the county.

You need a map of your district. It should be a large map and hung in a prominent place in your headquarters so everybody can see where the boundary lines are. Most cities, townships, counties, and governmental units have maps of their particular jurisdictions. These maps are usually produced at public expense by some department officially charged with that responsibility, such as the county engineer, the tax assessor, or the city planning office. They are readily available for a small fee, and early on in your campaign you will need to get one. Actually, you will need at least two, so get some extra copies of the map.

Your election district may cross jurisdictions. It may take in parts of two suburbs or two counties, so you may have to go to two or more offices to obtain a complete map of your district. In my court district there are fourteen counties, so I have to get fourteen different county maps, which takes some effort, but there is no way around this requirement. There is no substitute for a district map. You must have a complete and accurate map of your entire election district.

Once you have the map, take it to the elections office and look at the official boundaries of your district. Take a highlighter and carefully, street by street, highlight the perimeter of your district so that the area of your district is distinctly marked out. You might be running for an office that corresponds exactly to the official map. If you are in a citywide race, the city limits as they appear on the map are the perimeter, but you still have some work to do.

After you have the perimeter, take a highlighter and mark the boundaries of each ward, precinct, and voting place. It is helpful if you use different colors for color coding in marking out these intradistrict areas. Later on in this book we are going to tell you how you win an election one precinct at a time. To do that you have to have a precinct map for every precinct.

As we said above, you really need two maps. The first map is marked and color coded and hung up in your headquarters for ready reference for every worker and volunteer. The other map is used for producing precinct maps. Local campaigns are won precinct by precinct, so you will need a map of each precinct. Suppose, for example, you get a volunteer in Ward 1 Precinct A who offers to pass out literature and get people to put up yard signs. If you give that volunteer a list of registered voters, and a street map, that volunteer is better able to do what you want.

The individual precinct maps are as important as the headquarters maps, but you will pretty much have to produce these yourself. One way to make these precinct maps is to cut up the large district map. Once you have the perimeter and all the intradistrict lines marked out, you cut up the map along those lines and make photocopies of each precinct map. It helps if these precinct maps are enlarged because the official maps are often detailed and the detail does not stand out unless it is enlarged. Most copiers will do enlargements, or you can easily get an enlargement by going to a copier service. Get several copies of each precinct; you will find that they come in handy.

Another way to make up your precinct maps is to use one of the several map programs on CD-ROM. Delorme's Street Atlas USA has an excellent one with every street in the country reduced down to a scale of one inch equals 500 feet. It even shows the address numbers for each block. You can make precise, detailed precinct maps from these programs. These usually cost about $50 but are fairly popular, and you may have a volunteer who already has the program who can make maps for you. Google Maps and MapQuest also have good maps that can be used to create your precinct maps.

Having done the geography by obtaining one large headquarters map and several smaller but enlarged precinct maps, you now have to do the demography.

DEMOGRAPHY

"Who are the people in my district?" is another pretty basic question. Demography is about people. Demography is the data about people and how they live, which is gathered by census takers and mass marketers—like family size, average income, ethnic background, and so forth. If you are running for office, you are interested in local community and probably know a lot about it. But you don't get elected by assuming that you know a lot, you get elected by finding out what you don't know and knowing more than your opponent.

This is where census district information becomes invaluable. The U.S. Census Bureau has superimposed a grid over the entire country, dividing it up into blocks, which used to be called census tracts but are now called census districts. All the information the Census Bureau gathers about home ownership, age, educational levels, household income, and so forth is taken by census district, and then the information from all the districts is added together to create the national census data. Just as the national census can tell you a lot about the United States, the local census data can tell you a lot about the neighborhood you plan to run in.

At the U.S. Census Bureau website (www.census.gov) you can click on American FactFinder, type in a zip code, and all sorts of information will pop up. There is the usual stuff about age and home ownership and so forth but also a lot of very specialized information which might be helpful to your campaign. The data in the zip code area where I grew up shows:

Female householder, no husband present: 2,485 (13.7 percent)

The data in the zip code area where I now live shows:

Female householder, no husband present: 1,317 (6.07 percent)

You can probably make an inference about me based on just those two figures.

You will be amazed at all the information census data contains, and I am willing to bet that no matter how familiar you are with your home turf there is something new to be learned from looking at your local census data.

While census district data contains an awful lot of information, much of it is not very useful, like the number of bathrooms per household, but just looking through the census district data can provide some important insights. If one area has 2.5 bathrooms per household, it is probably an upscale neighborhood and the people who live there will vote differently from the people who live in an area where there are only 1.2 bathrooms per household. You can make some solid inferences about your district from a review of the census data. What inferences to make, which of the data is important, depends on your local race and conditions. Look for data that seems to be relevant to your particular race, either generally or specifically.

For example, it is well known that older people, church members, and homeowners tend to vote in greater numbers than young people, nonchurchgoers, and renters. Generally speaking, people with incomes or education levels at or below the median level tend to vote Democratic. On the other hand, people with higher educations have higher incomes and pay more taxes, and they tend to lean toward the Republicans. When you study the census district data and learn about all these general characteristics of the people in your district, you have a kind of satellite photograph. Census data will indicate the concentrations of certain groups of people, but this is only general information.

You have to examine this general information in light of how it will affect your run for office. We discussed making a

careful review of election statistics in Chapter 2 and the way
to pick a target number of votes needed to win. If you compare
the voting statistics in your district with the comparable demographic data for that area, you will have an even better idea of
where the votes are in your district.

Suppose, for example, the census data shows an upscale,
well educated, upper-income community that ordinarily ought
to be Republican, but the voting statistics show a strong
Democratic voting record. On checking further, you find the
area is heavily Jewish and Jewish voters tend to be more liberal, particularly on social issues. A liberal Democratic candidate will want to reach that liberal enclave. Another example
might be a blue-collar neighborhood with a history of strong
Democratic voting but that has 72 percent home ownership. If
there is an issue in the race that will affect property taxes or
real estate values, like sewer assessments or zoning changes,
these people are more likely to vote as homeowners than as
Democrats. A Republican candidate who has studied the data
and knows the area can exploit that opening and get votes
even in a heavily Democratic area.

Census districts do not coincide with political boundaries, so you may have to page through several of them to get
complete information, but it really does not take a lot of time.
You do not have to hunt through a lot of material, because the
significant data, the interesting and relevant local facts, leap
out at you.

While it may take an hour or two to do this kind of analysis,
you really should take the time to do this for two very good reasons. One is that it will make you a better candidate, because
the more you know about the people and how they live, the
better able you will be to reach out to them for their votes.

The second reason is more philosophical, but perhaps also
more important. The whole idea of this book is that public service is a public trust. If you are going to represent the people
of your district and their interests, you have a duty to learn as
much as you can about them. There are enough boobs who

think they know it all already holding public office. Don't be one of them. There is a really good chance you will be elected, and this census district data will not only help you win, it will make you a better informed public servant.

Geography and demography are important, but keep in mind the admonition that all politics is local, and local conditions vary. There is a precinct in New York City that consists, in its entirety, of the top half of one large apartment building inhabited by upscale, white-collar types. There is another precinct in South Dakota that encompasses several hundred square miles and is so sparsely populated that you could stand in the middle of it and fire a cannon in any direction and not hit any of the farmers or ranchers who live there.

You have to adapt what we say here to the specific electoral district you are running in. Our specific suggestions about drawing lines on the map and so forth may not apply exactly to your race because each district is different. What we say about knowing your local geography and demography, however, does apply no matter where you live. Regardless of the kind of district you are running in, you must know the "where" and "who." Where will I campaign? Who will vote for me?

These are basic questions, and you must know the answers to them almost from the very start of your campaign.

One final point is to look at the electoral history of the area. Neighborhoods don't change too fast, so the strategies from previous elections for that exact seat may give you insight into what works and what doesn't. Along with "who" and "where," there is always the "how," and this is where having an old hand becomes important.

→ 6 ←

TALKING TO AN OLD HAND

In theory, there is no difference between theory and practice, but in practice there is.
—Jan L. A. van de Snepscheut,
computer scientist, and Yogi Berra, baseball player

D o you know what absolute silence is? It's Dick Cheney and George W. Bush telling war stories. Veterans like to talk of their experiences, so much so that the phrase "war stories" has come to be a metaphor for an experienced person telling neophytes about the way things were and the way things are.

Telling war stories is not limited to the military. In almost every human occupation, institution, or endeavor, there is usually some old hand who has been around for a long time and who has learned a thing or two about the business. If you take a new job someplace, one of the best things you can do is find some long-term employee who knows the ropes and who can explain the intricacies of that operation.

Politics is no different. There are lots of veterans of the political wars who have been at it for a long time and who have learned from their experiences. One of the best things you can do in planning your campaign is to talk to one of these old hands. They have learned a lot, and you can benefit from their sense of political judgment.

As the old saying goes, "Good judgment comes from experience. Experience comes from not using good judgment." There are two ways you can learn about politics. One is to make all the mistakes yourself. The other is to talk to someone who has already made all the mistakes and learn how to avoid at least some of them. Avoiding mistakes is one part of experience; the other parts are knowing what works and knowing how to do things well. Not only can the old hand guide you away from blunders, he or she can direct your campaign into winning strategies.

A political old hand can be a former candidate, an officeholder, or a longtime worker in political campaigns. If you want to know what it is like to run for a seat on the village council, for example, one of the most likely people to ask is someone who has already run for that council seat. Do not be deterred by the fact that the former candidate didn't win. Win or lose, he probably learned some valuable lessons and has insights into the peculiarities of that kind of race.

Someone who has run for the office and won is, of course, in a position to tell you how it is done. More exactly, he can tell you how it was done one time in one race, but knowing what worked before is helpful in deciding what might work this time. The successful candidate does not have to be one who ran for the office you're trying for but can be someone who ran for a similar office.

For example, a mayor runs throughout the entire city, while councilmen usually run from wards. Sometimes, however, a councilman will run at large, so that race is very much like the mayoralty race. A person who has run for council at large will have some good ideas on how to run for mayor, and vice versa.

The third, and perhaps the most important, category of old hand is the veteran worker—someone who has not been a candidate or held office but has worked in several campaigns over the years. While a candidate can tell you about his own campaigns, his experience is generally limited to those campaigns. An old hand who has worked in a lot of different races has seen more and done more and has a better overall perspective of how things are done.

Whatever kind of old hand you latch on to, be sure to listen to what he or she tells you. You are the candidate and you have to make the final decision, but the situation is like with a football coach and his assistants. The coach has the final say-so on what play to call, but he is a damn fool if he doesn't listen to what the offensive coordinator has to say.

In the planning stages of the campaign, you have to first find an old hand. It is not all that hard, but it's very important to find one to talk with, one whom you can ask a lot of questions. Ask around. Ask someone in your party or neighborhood. You ought to know your neighbors well enough so that one of them can put you on to a person who is known to be politically involved.

What kind of questions? Well, the very first question to ask is if he will help you in winning. Having an experienced person participate in your planning and strategy sessions is a real advantage. Having an old hand as campaign manager, or scheduler, or volunteer coordinator puts an experienced person in a job that requires a lot of decision making. But even if the veteran is just a volunteer campaign worker, it is very handy to have one available to give advice and suggestions.

Below is a list of questions you should ask the old hand about running in your local area.

1. What works?
2. What kind of issue motivates the local voters?
3. What are some of the peculiarities of this area?
4. What doesn't work, or what turns the local voters off?
5. What kinds of problems or mistakes do first-time candidates usually make with their nominating petitions or financing statements?
6. What do you think of my review of the election statistics?
7. Where, in what neighborhoods, do we need to work to win this?

8. How strong is my opponent? How hard will it be to beat him?
9. How can we raise money?
10. What kind of fund-raisers are most effective?
11. Where do we find volunteers?
12. How do we use them to our best advantage?
13. Where do local voters get their information about candidates?
14. Which is better—radio or local cable television?
15. How effective is newspaper advertising?
16. Do mailings work? What kind?
17. What do you think of yard signs, bumper stickers, and so forth?

Some of you more perceptive readers are probably thinking to yourselves right now, "Wait a minute! This list is nothing more than a rehash of many of the chapters in this book." That's the point exactly. The information we are giving you in this book is of a general nature and will work generally speaking, but you have to know the ins and outs of local conditions. You can learn a lot from a book about fly-fishing, but if you want to actually catch fish in the New River in West Virginia or along the Yellowstone River in Montana, you had better talk to a local, old-time fisherman because he is the one who knows where the best fishing spot is.

All politics is local, and you have to ask what works and what doesn't in your locale. For example, there was a small Midwestern county with the population almost equally divided between rural residents and the people who lived in the county seat. The rural people were conservative, mostly farmers, who had lived all their lives in the county. The city people were more liberal. Many had moved in along with a high-tech factory, which had been built a few years before, and were viewed by longtime residents as outsiders. A woman, one of the newcomers, decided to run for a county office and although under that state's election laws she could have used her maiden name or her married name, she chose to use her hyphenated married name, Mary Smith-Jones.

Her choice of the hyphenated name irrevocably doomed her campaign from the start. Although she did not realize it, her choice of name turned the rural voters off. They might have listened to what Mary Jones or Mary Smith had to say, but her choice of the hyphenated name was like saying to the rural voter, "Don't vote for me—I'm one of those liberal outsiders!" Her opponent had most of the rural vote in his pocket and worked hard in the city, and won. If she had talked to a local old hand, she would have avoided this disastrous mistake in that county. If she had talked to a knowledgeable political old hand, someone like Hillary Clinton, the wife of the candidate, she would have been advised not to use the hyphenated name at least until after the election. Senator Hillary Rodham Clinton is an old hand at politics.

In the United States, there are over 3,300 counties and tens of thousands of cities that are further subdivided into hundreds of thousands of neighborhoods. This book cannot tell you how to run in each one. Running in the French Quarter in New Orleans is going to be a lot different than running in the Seattle suburb of Auburn, and frankly, we cannot tell you what these differences are. But we can tell you that somewhere in the French Quarter, and in Auburn, and in your district, there is some old hand who has been around the block and who knows how to win in that area.

One final point about these political old hands: don't take them for granted. You have to campaign for their support just as you would for any voter, perhaps more so since they are very astute politically. When you ask for their help, they will be pleased that you have the good sense to realize how important they are to an effective campaign, but still they are going to give you the once over. They are very much interested in good government and good candidates. They will work hard for someone they like, for someone who supports the policies they support. They will work hard for a candidate who has a good chance of winning and will enhance those chances. But you have to show them, first, that you are that kind of candidate. In the first chapter we said you will be asked what your candidacy is about and to be ready with an answer. The old hand will most certainly ask you that question, too.

If you've done the preliminary work described in the preceding chapters, he will be impressed. If you listen to the old hand and learn how much he knows about local conditions, you will be impressed. You will begin to understand why we recommend having an old hand as an important part of a winning campaign.

7

CAMPAIGN THEME AND STRATEGY

Politics is a profession: a serious, complicated and, in its way, a noble one.

—Dwight D. Eisenhower

Too bad the only people who know how to run the country are busy driving cabs and cutting hair.

—George Burns

A retired master sergeant who did thirty years in an artillery company often showed up to volunteer on many campaigns. He had a favorite saying. "In the army, the first thing they taught me to do was to point the cannon in the right direction." This tongue-in-cheek observation makes the point that, in the artillery, you begin your planning by thinking about the end result. The same is true for a political campaign. You begin by planning for the end result—you pick your target, and aim at that.

If you have done as we suggested in the earlier chapters, you have the statistics and an idea of how many votes it will take to win. You know the area and the kind of people who live there. You have done the research on the office, the issues, and the relevant facts. Now you have to put it all together into a coherent campaign strategy.

Every campaign is different, with different kinds of problems that must be met with different kinds of strategies. Begin by preparing a menu list of the various factors that are applicable to all campaigns, and then make a list of local factors that are likely to affect the outcome. When you have a list of all possible factors, you select one from column A and one from column B (as in a Chinese restaurant), to decide what is important in your particular race.

For example, you might use these criteria for assessing the office you plan to run for:

Column A:
A. High-profile office
B. Low-profile office, voter fatigue
C. Policy-making office
D. Budget-spending office
E. Administrative office
F. Service-to-public office

These criteria might be used for assessing the district's makeup and the kind of voters it has:

Column B:
A. Partisan, your party
B. Partisan, the other party
C. Heavily independent
D. Older (younger) neighborhood
E. Ethnic (nonethnic) neighborhood
F. Blue (white) collar
G. Mixed district

Then you must analyze your opponent's and your candidate's strengths and weaknesses:

Column C:
A. Incumbent is popular or unpopular
B. Open seat—no incumbent
C. Opponent is well known with high name identification
D. Candidate has poor name identification
E. The other side is (not) well financed
F. Our side is (not) well financed

The kind of race you will be in will definitely affect your planning and strategy:

Column D:
A. Two-way race
B. Three-way race
C. Top three vote getters win
D. Contested primary, crossover voting not allowed
E. Contested primary, crossover voting allowed
F. Off-year general election with a low turnout
G. Presidential year with a big turnout
H. Special election

These are the general characteristics of any election, but your election will probably have some special features, like a local scandal, which also should be added to your list of factors that will affect the outcome of the election. Analyzing these local factors is where advice from the old hand can be especially invaluable.

In the appendix there is a complete outline of campaign strategy that was used successfully in an actual election. This sample was included to show you what an overall campaign plan might look like. It is only an example, but you can use it when you sit down to prepare your own campaign strategy.

This might be a good time to turn to Appendix A and see the discussion of the overall strategy as it was done in that campaign. You will have to prepare a written outline of campaign strategy very similar to the one in the appendix.

As you can see from the example, it is not enough to say that this is a race for clerk of a municipal court. All the criteria above, and more, have to be factored in. In planning the campaign, you have to analyze and write down a list of the variables in your electoral district. For example,

This is a race for assemblywoman, which is a high-profile office because of budget cuts the legislature made.

It will be a two-way race, in an off-year election, in a district that is 60 percent blue collar, with a strong Polish–Slavic ethnic makeup. Party registration is about 40 percent Democrat, and 30 percent Republican, and the older voters tend to vote the straight-party ticket. The younger voters are more likely to be Independents, but young women who are registered Democrats tend to vote for women candidates regardless of party affiliation.

The opponent, a man, has never run for office before and is not too well financed, but he has a popular political name and will get help from the Democratic Party. Your candidate, a Republican woman, has one term as city councilwoman and is fairly popular in her ward, but that ward makes up only 16 percent of the district.

This type of analysis tells where to point the cannon, doesn't it? This analysis almost preordains what she has to do if she is going to win. First, she has to be sure that all the neighbors who know and like her as a councilwoman will vote for her. Getting out the vote in her home ward will be a primary tactic in the overall strategy.

Second, she has to get the straight-ticket Republicans to vote for her in their usual numbers. Since her opponent has a popular political name, she has a name identification problem. She has to make sure the Republicans know her name as the Republican candidate.

But even with her own ward, and the Republican vote, she cannot win. She has to try to get a majority of the Independents, or cut into the opponent's strength with younger Democratic women. Or perhaps both. This is where the campaign theme comes in.

In 1992, at President Clinton's campaign headquarters in Little Rock, there was a prominently displayed sign which read, "The economy, stupid!" That was an insider's joke indicating that for Clinton's campaign, the answer to any question about the campaign was the economy. The Clinton people thought the economy was the most important issue and they used it, successfully of course, as the polestar of all campaign activity. Clinton started out in New Hampshire talking about the economy, and he was still hitting that theme the day before the election. He won in no small part because he focused his entire campaign on that single theme while Bush's campaign remained unfocused.

In 2004, Bush II had the focus while Senator Kerry floundered. The war in Iraq was an issue and President Bush hammered on the theme that it was part of the war on terror. And while Bush hammered, Kerry yammered—about maybe withdrawing, or maybe staying, or maybe something else. In 2006 the Democrats made the war their issue, focused on getting out, and won control of both houses.

You will need that same kind of focus in your campaign. You will need a theme, a simple word or phrase that epitomizes what you and your campaign are all about. You can expect from a reporter, or someone at a meet-the-candidates night, a question like this: "What is your campaign really about?" You have to be ready with a short, precise answer. "My campaign is about caring for people." Or, "This campaign is about tax fairness."

Selecting the campaign theme should be done by sitting down with your supporters in a strategy session and going through the factors as previously described. Kick some ideas around and see if you can't come up with that one word or phrase that says it all in a nutshell.

In our example, winning depends on reaching the Independents and the young Democratic women voters. If one of those target voters came up to you and asked that question, what would your answer be? That answer should be your campaign theme. For example, "My whole campaign is about better schools." This is one way to reach your target voters. This identifies you as the education candidate.

We are not suggesting that you abandon your principles or campaign on something that is not important to you. Don't pick an issue you don't believe in just because you think it will get you votes. If you think schools are important but are keenly interested in the environment and think this is a more important issue, then use that as your theme. You cannot be all things to all people, and government is ultimately nothing more than setting priorities. You pick your priority as a candidate, and if it is as important to the voters in your district, you will win.

Your theme identifies what your campaign, and you, stand for. Senator Dole said that he wanted to be the education president, and the environment president, and the family values president, and the foreign policy president. President Bill Clinton, on the other hand, talked mostly about the economy and how well it was doing. If asked about education, Clinton always worked his answer around to some comment about how hard it was for people to send their kids to college without a good job. If asked about the environment, he talked about how the economy could be improved and jobs created by developing new environmental technologies. He always came back to the economy.

You have to have that same kind of thematic single-mindedness. If you're "about better schools" and someone asks about welfare reform, tell them your position honestly. But then add that there is no sense in talking about welfare reform, or getting people off welfare unless those people have a good enough education to be productive workers. If someone asks about new roads as promoting economic development, tell them you are for the new roads and for economic development, but nobody is going to build a new factory in this city unless they know they can hire from a trained, well-educated labor pool.

As a candidate, you have to stand for something. That something can be a negative, like opposition to the tax levy, or a positive, like being for a new high school, but you must take a principled stand and identify yourself in terms of that principle. That principle is your campaign theme. The theme must recur over and over in your campaign. In later chapters, we will talk about integrating that theme into your literature and advertising, but the first step is for you to select the theme. Don't wait for the reporter's question. Ask yourself: What is my campaign all about? The answer is your campaign theme.

Strategy is asking: How do I win this? Your theme is asking: Why do I want to win this? The answer to the first question is complicated and involves many people and varying factors. The answer to the second is straightforward and involves only the candidate. If the candidate has his message clear in his own head, that message will come across to voters during the campaign. That message, your statement of principle, is your campaign theme.

8

PARTY, NONPARTISAN, AND INDEPENDENT CANDIDATES

Mothers all want their sons to grow up to be president, but they don't want them to become politicians in the process.
—John F. Kennedy

Every candidate has to decide whether to run as a party candidate or as an Independent. Before you make this decision, let's talk about politics for a bit. Political parties and politics in general are not well thought of in this country, which is odd when you think about it. Imagine if someone was talking about a doctor and what a great surgeon he was, and someone else said, "Yeah, but I saw him once, and he was dirty. He had blood all over his hands!" Surgery is a bloody business because blood is the vital fluid of the body. Politics is the vital fluid of our democracy, and like surgery, politics is a gory, messy business when you look at it up close. Everybody is in favor of Democracy with a capital D but against politics, although it is politics that makes the democracy work.

The reformers and the do-gooders have been at our democracy trying to make it less political, and they have succeeded to some extent. As a result, our governmental institutions, whether local, state, or national, have become progressively more removed and unresponsive to the needs of ordinary citizens.

The post office is a concrete example. It used to be a politically controlled organization. The ordinary mailmen were nonpolitical, but every postmaster and his assistants—the middle-management types—were answerable to the local congressman. They were expected to support and work for the reelection of the congressman who appointed them. If the congressman was unhappy with the postmaster, or a new congressman was elected, the postmaster was fired.

When the political post office was replaced by the nonpolitical U.S. Postal Service, an independent, public corporation, it became just another bureaucracy, unanswerable to the public. Service has gone to hell, prices have risen, and the ordinary workers who want to do a good job are caught up in a system where only following regulation counts and actually delivering the mail to people is, in a sense, irrelevant. From my discussions with postal workers, they are as frustrated by the bigwigs in this bureaucracy as the customers are.

Some might not agree with this assessment, but historically, nonpolitical bureaucracies become unresponsive, and people become alienated as their government and institutions become more nonpolitical. I would guess that if you are considering running for local office, you are motivated to some extent by a feeling that your local government is not as responsive, or caring, or even aware of the feelings of many of the voters.

"Politics" has become a dirty word, and "politician" is an epithet, but it is the elected officeholder, the politician, who has gone out and met the people in his district. He has talked to them, and listened to them. He has proposed ideas, programs, and solutions to local problems. He has convinced a majority of the voters that he can do the job, and if he doesn't, the voters reserve the right to vote him out of office and frequently exercise that right.

If you run for office, you are a politician. Do not lie to yourself and say you are acting only as a concerned citizen, or a statesman, or in the interest of public service. Don't try to be nonpolitical, or apolitical, or some other euphemism. Be what you are: be a politician. It is our elected politicians, like Washington, Jefferson, Lincoln, the Roosevelts, Eisenhower, and Kennedy, who made this country great, and every one of them was an accomplished politician skilled at getting votes. Washington and Jefferson both bought barrels of whiskey to provide free drinks for their supporters on election day.

Perhaps an even more pejorative term than "politician" is the double damning "party politician." In the minds of many, political parties are conspiracies—wicked and evil institutions whose only function is to serve special interests. In fact, political parties are nothing more than groups of people who hold the same general philosophy.

Here is a test. Suppose an employee makes $10 an hour and the state imposes a 6 percent worker's compensation insurance premium charge on every hour worked. Who pays this worker's compensation premium?

A. The 60 cents per hour is paid by the employer. As a mandatory benefit, it is a cost that comes out of the employer's profits.

B. The 60 cents is paid by the employee, as a part of wages. Since a wage earner must produce goods or services worth $10 plus 60 cents or be fired, the 60 cents is wages that would otherwise be paid to the employee.

Some readers will pick A and others B, but regardless of the choice, there is an affinity among all the As and among all the Bs. They tend to think alike not only about an issue like this but about life in general. This affinity or consensus among a like-minded group of people is, when applied to government, what makes a political party.

You have the right to think the way you think, and that will get you exactly one vote—your own. Politics is getting the votes of others, however, so candidates seek out other voters who think as they think. When there is a cluster of like-thinking people, that is the foundation of a political party—a common philosophy of government.

In practice, of course, party politics is a rough-and-tumble business full of posturing, greed, ambition, and egomaniacal vendettas. Within every party, whether the great national parties or the local parties, there are factions, disputes, and controversy over policies and candidates. And both parties are subject to political Alzheimer's—where you forget everything but the grudges. For all their faults, and in spite of all the dissension, basic philosophical principles are the glue that holds a political party together. When the chips are down, when faced with a great social or moral issue, the Democrats will revert to their principles and react like Democrats, and the Republicans will react in accord with theirs.

Simply put, the political party is at root one of the most principled institutions in our society. It used to be that you could not run without strong party support, but the reformers have changed all that. Now, particularly in elections for federal office, it's all money and television, and, as might be expected, the government is most responsive to the people with money.

We spent a great deal of time discussing political parties and whether to run as a party candidate or as an Independent, but before that decision can be made, there is still one other point that has to be mentioned—the difference between partisan and nonpartisan elections. Generally speaking, a partisan election is one where the candidate's party affiliation is indicated on the ballot and they campaign as a member of that party. A nonpartisan race is one where there is no affiliation indicated on the ballot.

While that simple, theoretical distinction applies to many elective offices, the reality is often quite different. The purpose behind having nonpartisan elections is to eliminate the political parties' influence on the election. Whether the goal of keeping party politics out of nonpartisan elections is ever accomplished or even desirable is the subject of continuing debate.

Some elections for certain offices are genuinely nonpartisan—for example, a school board race where neither party actively seeks or supports candidates. Other offices are nonpartisan in name only, and each party recruits and supports candidates to fill those offices. Judicial races are often officially nonpartisan, but actually very partisan in the way they are conducted, with each party publicly supporting and endorsing their judicial candidates. Many elections in cities operating under a charter have only nonpartisan offices, yet the candidates for mayor or city councilmen and councilwomen divide themselves along party lines.

You have to determine if the office you are running for is listed as partisan or nonpartisan. If it is nonpartisan, you then have to determine if it is really nonpartisan or if the parties are actively involved in helping candidates. Keep in mind that partisan or nonpartisan, the techniques we describe here about campaigning and planning still apply.

Let us turn back now to one major planning decision, whether to run as a party candidate or as an Independent, and if as a party candidate, from what party.

We recommend against running as an Independent. While there may be some merit in saying you are not tied to any party or ideology, such a declaration of independence often leaves the voter wondering what you do stand for. Everyone knew that Ross Perot was against the Republican president and the Democratic Congress, but he failed dismally to establish what he was for.

Being a party candidate does not mean you agree with everything or everyone involved in that party. With the huge number of "defining issues" or "hot-button issues" floating around today, it is ridiculous to think that two clear-cut partisan positions can be staked out on every issue on which all the members of the same party can completely agree. A few hours of viewing the Sunday morning television panel discussions, the television commentaries, or C-SPAN will convince you of that. Nobody is tied to any party ideology, and that is what makes party politics the confusing, contradictory system it is.

Party affiliation is often a function of your upbringing: people tend to vote the way their parents voted. As a candidate, you have to assess your basic political beliefs. Do not hesitate to reevaluate your political party affiliation. Some people believe that their party has lost touch with its basic philosophy or that the party is on the wrong track. Your initial decision to characterize yourself as an R or a D or an Independent need not be carved in stone. Independent voters often become party candidates.

Many people have switched parties. Ronald Reagan was a Democrat when he was president of the actor's union in the 1950s. In the 1990s, starting with the Republicans regaining control of both the House and Senate, there was a lot of realignment. In Florida, ten state legislators and one state senator changed sides. In 2006, Senator Lieberman lost the Democratic primary but then won an Independent in the general. It can be done.

Beware, however, of switching your party affiliation with the intent of running for office as a recent convert. Americans distrust a turncoat generally, and many party people will not work for a person who seems to choose his affiliation based on ambition rather than principle. John Connally, the Democratic governor of Texas, became a Republican but was always perceived by a lot of people in both parties as being motivated only by ambition. Shortly after he switched, I attended a dinner where on the table in front of the podium they had a ten-gallon hat sitting on top of a pair of snakeskin cowboy boots. The speaker told the audience that "this is John Connally without all the BS."

Aside from the political disadvantages from switching parties, many states have laws that impose restrictions on people running for office in one party when they have recently voted as a member of another party. Check this out. If you are not really affiliated with a party, and you only voted in that party's primary once as a favor to a friend, you might still be regarded as a member of that party under your state's election laws.

Running as an Independent is difficult, which is why we recommend against it. You might think there is some advantage because you do not have to run in a primary or because in a three-way race you need fewer votes to win. The reality is usually that if a candidate cannot win a primary, he cannot win a general election either. And in a three-way race, the Independent just takes votes away from the party candidate closest to his position, and the other party wins. A conservative who runs as an Independent will split the vote with the Republican, and the liberal Democrat wins. Or vice versa. It is hard for an Independent to win.

We have suggested running as a party candidate for very sound philosophical reasons, but the practical reasons are even more compelling. It is easier to run as a party candidate, and easier to win. All parties, even minority parties, are looking for attractive candidates who will work hard and who can win. If you are thinking about running, talk to your local party chairman and ask for his help and advice. Local politics is like a baseball farm team—always looking for some promising young rookie. If it finds one who is willing to be a candidate and take on some entrenched incumbent from the other party, it will be most helpful.

The local parties have an established infrastructure of experienced people who can be a great source of volunteers for your campaign. We talked about the importance of getting campaign advice from an old hand, and local parties are full of these knowledgeable people whose advice and help can be indispensable. If you are in one of those races that is non-partisan in name only, the party can still be quite helpful.

One very significant factor is the party's strength in your district. It is sometimes said that in local politics people vote for the best man or woman rather than because he or she is a member of a certain political party. There is some truth to this because the voters are interested in the well-being of their local government and more knowledgeable about what is going on in the community. This is perhaps one of the most encouraging features of local races. You must realize, however, that many of the voters do vote for the candidate from their party.

For example, West Virginia is very Democratic. The 1998 West Virginia roster of elected officeholders shows two (of two) Democrat U.S. senators and three (of three) Democrat U.S. representatives, or five (of six) statewide Democrat office-holders. The state senate has twenty-six Ds to eight Rs, and in the House the Democrats outnumber the Republicans seventy-four to twenty-six. Utah is just the opposite, with seventy-five Republican legislators versus twenty-nine Democrats.

It is not impossible for a Republican candidate to win in West Virginia—Governor Underwood is a Republican—nor for a Democrat in Utah—Attorney General Jan Graham is a Democrat. Nonetheless, the party affiliation in your district may give you a distinct advantage, or it might be a burdensome disadvantage, depending on the area's party registration figures. You have to take this into account.

In some areas, however, party affiliation may be nearly equal, or the Independents might even outnumber both party registrations put together. You must have a good understanding of what you are facing and include the party registration figures in your district when formulating your campaign strategy.

A candidate for public office will be guided by both political ideology and political reality. If you are a serious candidate, you cannot ignore the predominant party affiliation in your particular district, but you cannot change your politics merely to win an election either. If you decide to make a serious attempt to win the election, we strongly suggest that you affiliate with the party most closely in tune with your values, and that you seek to be that party's candidate.

Finally, a word about write-in candidates. A write-in candidate is a candidate whose name is not printed on the ballot. In order to cast a vote for a write-in candidate, the voter must physically handwrite the candidate's name on the ballot. In an age of electronic and machine voting, write-in candidates have an even smaller chance to win than they had during the paper and pencil ballot era.

We will not devote much time to a discussion of write-in candidates. On occasion, a man who has never played football in high school or college will walk on to the practice field of a professional football team and be so good he is offered a contract. Write-in candidates are the walk-ons of politics, and you have as much chance of winning as a write-in candidate as you have of getting a professional football contract. Actually, you might have a better shot at the football team, because I know of two football walk-ons but only one successful write-in.

The kind of election—partisan or nonpartisan—the kind of candidate you should be—party candidate or Independent—each of these factors has to be considered in planning your run for office.

9

COMPUTERS: USING THEM IN THE CAMPAIGN

Technology makes it possible for people to gain control over everything, except technology.

—John Tudor

U sing a computer is not unlike dealing with a recalcitrant teenager. No matter what you ask them to do, you either get an evasive answer or another question in return. But when they actually do something, they go at it with such vigor and enthusiasm that they often do more than you want them to.

This chapter covers computers and how to use them in a local campaign, but a word about computers in general is in order. The problem with writing about computers is that almost everything you write may be out of date by the time it is published. But even if there are no eternal verities in the field of computers, in the field of politics the strategies and tactics for winning a local election do not change that much. This chapter describes two aspects about using computers in a political race. One is getting and using a simple computer in your campaign headquarters. The other is getting a computer person—that is, a volunteer who really knows how to make the best use of computers.

To summarize, this chapter makes two points: You need a low-tech computer for your campaign headquarters. You need a high-tech computer person for planning.

Let's talk about the low-tech headquarters computer first.

LOW-TECH: THE CAMPAIGN COMPUTER

Begin your computer planning by making a decision as to whether you need a computer at all. While computers are efficient in handling large amounts of data, like all machines they involve a certain amount of time and money in setup costs. In a very small campaign, it may be more efficient to do everything by hand using volunteers. As the number of voters you are trying to reach grows, the use of a computer in your campaign becomes more important. As a rule of thumb, if your target number as described in Chapter 2 is 1,000 or less, or if the total number of registered voters in your district is less than 5,000, you may not need a computer at all. If you have double these numbers—a target number of 2,000 or 10,000 registered voters—it would be hard to get by without a computer. If your number is greater than that, having a computer is an absolute necessity, and you have to find a computer whiz who can set up a computer to do the things you want and need to do.

When using computers in your campaign, I recommend that you get two of them—one, a kind of an old "station-wagon" type that will be used in the headquarters, and one, a super-splenderific Porsche type, to be used by the computer person for planning, graphics, and so on. It doesn't matter where the second computer is as long as your expert has ready access to it. I will talk later about the computer person's duties and using a state-of-the-art computer for planning and organizing, but first I'll talk about the computer you will need in your campaign headquarters.

Don't buy a headquarters computer. Any money you spend can be put to better use in advertising or mailing. You can probably get someone to loan or donate one to the campaign. This should be the computer expert's first task. He or she might have one you can use because people often keep their old computers even though they have upgraded their equipment. Computer-literate kids go off to college, leaving a computer sitting idle in their parents' home. Since they have so little trade-in value, there are a lot of out-of-date but still functional computers just lying around unused except as door stops. You will not be doing graphics at the headquarters, so a monochrome monitor is good enough for use in a local political campaign. A desktop computer is probably better than a laptop for the headquarters. As a matter of fact, a simpler, easier-to-use system may be better. Your headquarters volunteers may be only somewhat familiar with computers. Word Perfect for Windows 6.1 can do a lot more than Word Perfect 5.1, but you don't need a computer that can do a lot of things. You need a computer that can be operated by anyone and do a few things well. Your computer guru ought to be able to scrounge one up. Always check the donated computer for files that may have been left on the hard drive, such as porn.

You will need a printer, too; don't buy one of them, either. There are a lot of them around, too, particularly the old-fashioned black-and-white printers. Many people go to color printers when they upgrade, so you ought to be able to get the use of a good black-and-white printer that, even if it is a bit slower than today's printers, will serve your campaign needs. If you can get a color printer, well and good, but color is not necessary for the basic headquarters tasks of making lists and forms and printing letters or news releases. A monochrome laser printer produces professional-looking results with the cheapest cost per page.

The campaign headquarters computer has to be accessible to anyone who might be working there, so if you are getting a donated computer make sure that a password is not necessary to boot up, or have the password written down and attached to the monitor so anyone can enter it. But with such open access, don't keep any sensitive information on the computer. If someone lends you the use of a printer, be sure they also send along at least one backup printer cartridge; if they don't, buy one and keep it on hand.

A fax machine can be a real blessing in a small campaign, and I mention them here because they are related to computer office equipment. A fax machine is very useful for getting information out, such as news releases, and if your district is larger, the fax machine provides an easy way to communicate. A fax can do double duty as a copier for small jobs, since most of them also copy. Unlike computers, unfortunately, there are not many fax machines lying around idle, and being able to borrow a fax for a few months during the campaign is not all that easy. Having a fax is not an absolute necessity, but try to get one for your headquarters if you can.

Warning!

The loan of a computer, fax machine, or printer may constitute an in-kind donation, which, in some states, must be reported on your financial report. Check this out under your local law. ⟵

Word Processors.

The headquarters computer can be a simple machine; as long as it has a word processor program, it will serve. The major function of the headquarters computer is to do word processing—letters, forms, news releases, and so on—basic typing stuff. The computer will be used by various people, but almost any kind of word processor program will do. Most people who have experience with one word processor have a sufficient working knowledge of computer word processing functions in general so that they can adapt to whatever program you're using.

Your headquarters word processor will be used for a lot of campaign tasks besides typing letters and news releases. You can have the candidate's basic speech in memory ready to be modified for any speaking engagement. You can have position papers to print out if the need ever arises. The headquarters computer should be able to generate forms to be used in managing the campaign. For example, a volunteer card master form (see Appendix E) can be typed up and saved in memory long before you start recruiting volunteers.

From then on, whenever you need volunteer forms, it is simply a matter of calling up that file and hitting the Print key. Or, you may need a set of special instruction sheets for some tasks. For example, if your state has certain requirements for petition signing, when you give someone a petition to circulate, you should also give that person an instruction sheet that gives explicit directions on how to do it correctly. You may want to draft instructions addressing envelopes or on how to go door to door, and so on.

In the appendixes of this book and on the accompanying CD-ROM there are several sample campaign forms. All these forms, instructions, and worksheets should be modified to fit your particular situation and saved on the computer. Later in the campaign, any of them can be recalled in seconds.

Labels.

Part of your campaign is likely to involve mailing things to various groups—newspapers, volunteers, contributors, and so on. Having a set of preprinted adhesive address labels for each group may prove to be very handy.

During the race, you will probably compile a list of names and addresses so that you can contact those people at a future date. With a good label-making program, when the need to contact these people arises, you can simply call up the address label list on the computer, print out a set of address labels, and stick them on envelopes. When things get hectic—and campaigns always do—having these address labels prepared and available in a few minutes can be very helpful. If you go with the high-tech computer approach, a better way to make labels is to print them using your database program. One of the examples on the CD-ROM that accompanies this book provides more details.

There are various ways to make up these address label lists with relatively inexpensive label programs. Some word processor software systems have built-in label programs. Which one to use is a decision for the computer person and may depend on what kind of computer gets donated for the headquarters, but you should have some kind of system for making address labels. I like the Avery Label program software. It is relatively inexpensive (about $50) and easy to use. It is designed to be used with Avery labels, which are widely available. This is not a plug for Avery, per se, only that I have used it and it is good. Microsoft Word (version 6.0 or later) is a word processor program, not a label program per se, but it will do labels and just about anything else you might need. There are others that I have not used that are probably just as good.

Lists.

Sometimes having a computer with a database function can prove very helpful, because another thing you need the headquarters computer to do is to make lists, especially lists of people who share certain common characteristics. This is what is called "the database." A database is nothing more than a great list of names with some information about each name. All a relational database program does is find and sort out the names or information in the way you want. This is a bit of an oversimplification, but for campaign purposes, that is about all that it amounts to. A good relational database program is FileMaker Pro, but there are others that work well, too. The examples contained on the accompanying CD-ROM are made with FileMaker Pro 8.5.

For example, you will need computerized lists for, at minimum, these following five groups:

1. The media—newspapers, radio, television, etc.
2. Petition signers
3. Contributors
4. Precinct captains
5. Volunteers

You may need other lists, depending on the particular situation in your race or local circumstances (e.g., persons to whom expenditures have been made, persons to invite to your fund-raiser). Some of these lists will have to be further broken down into sublists, such as the volunteer list, that may look like this:

- telephoning
- addressing
- yard signs

I want to emphasize that the computerized list I am talking about here is the specialized list you prepare for your campaign. You may also need to get a computerized list of registered voters, but this list is so important that an entire chapter has been devoted to it—Chapter 18, "Getting a Good Mailing List."

HIGH-TECH: THE COMPUTER PERSON

Each chapter in this book is devoted to a separate task or special function that must be done to have a successful campaign. A person who is familiar with computers and what they can do may find it easier to use a computer to do a lot of the things suggested in this book. Many of them can be done, or can be done better, with the aid of a computer. Rather than injecting the use of computers into each chapter, as a matter of editorial choice I have decided to have one chapter on computers, and talk about how computers can be used to accomplish each of these essential tasks.

For example, in talking about the demography of your district I recommended that you take a look at the census districts for your area and suggested that you get that information at your local library. If you know how to find things on the Internet, you can get this data yourself at http://www.census.gov. As a matter of fact, if you go to the library, there is a good chance that they will not have the current census data on file on paper. They will have someone there to help you, to show you how to access the census website on their computer and get the data you need.

The fact that local libraries have someone to help you with computers demonstrates an important point. In organizing a local political campaign, having a computer is handy, but having the assistance of a good computer person is far more helpful. Unless you are good with computers yourself, you really ought to get a person to handle the use of computers in your campaign. If you are a candidate who is good with computers, you are going to need a good computer person as much as anyone, because as a candidate your time should be spent meeting and talking to people.

The most important criteria for a reliable computer person is not so much a knowledge of computers but a willingness to understand what you need the computer to do. Let me give an example, one not related to politics.

When I decided to computerize the court's operation, I looked at several systems and talked to different people, and they all started by telling us about how their system would do this, that, and the other thing. One guy, Charlie Collins, was entirely different. The first thing he did was to sit us down at a table and say, "What do you want your computer to do? I can get it to do almost anything, but the first step is for you to think about the things you want it to do." Charlie designed the best of all computer programs for us, one which does exactly what I want it to do.

You will have to find someone like Charlie, and since you are likely to be using the computer almost from the very beginning, you ought to have your computer person involved at the very earliest stages of planning your campaign. Fully a third of this book is devoted to planning because it is so crucial to success at the polls, so if you are going to use a computer it ought to be an integral part of the plan. The computer person—the one who will be integrating the computers into the campaign—ought to be brought on board early so that he or she knows just exactly what the computer system has to do.

Your campaign computer consultant must not only be knowledgeable about computers, but he or she also has to have a state-of-the-art setup—a fast computer, a scanner, a quality color printer, and software that works with graphics, databases, spreadsheets, and so forth. With top-of-the-line equipment and a good idea of what is needed, your computer consultant can add to your campaign's effectiveness.

Let's take the example used previously about getting demographic data. I recommended that a candidate be informed about the area he is campaigning in, and the census district data is fairly informative, but there is a lot more information available out there. A person who is used to rooting out things on the Internet can find a whole lot of information that may be helpful to the candidate. Where does your school district rank in per-pupil expenditures? What is the average number of police officers in a town your size? Information like this may not be vital, but if a candidate has a computer consultant who has searched and gathered this data, he may come across as a better, more informed candidate during a debate or a news conference—or even in just talking to voters.

Computers, and the things they can do, may make your campaign more polished. Below are some suggestions on how to use computers to add to your campaign. Some of them are quite minor, and some of them are more important, but all of them are useful and will add a little style to your race.

Website and E-Mail.

The Internet has gained universal acceptance for modern communication. No campaign, no matter how small, should be without a website and an e-mail account. The cost of obtaining a website is very small. Internet domain names can be purchased for about $15 per year. Donated website storage space can be used for your campaign, and the unique website name that you've chosen can be linked to anywhere using services such as dyndns.org for about $25 per year. Also, your computer guru will also set up e-mail accounts for all who need them. Most of your press releases and other quick communication will use e-mail which has largely supplanted fax for distributing time-sensitive information. Your computer guru will know how to design web pages for your campaign site or know someone who can do it. Just make sure that the finished product looks professional and conveys the most important facts that you want voters to know about you.

Letterhead.

You ought to have campaign stationery with the name of the campaign committee and all the ways you can be reached (e.g., work and home address; work, cell, and home phone; fax number; e-mail address). In some states, this information is required on all election materials, but even if it isn't you should include it. Computers can be used to design and print a good-looking letterhead, and this will create a good impression for the candidate. For small jobs, such as a few hundred

---

COMMITTEE TO ELECT BROWN

P. O. Box 1111   740-555-1234

Irving, TN 32109   Fax 740-555-6789

www.YourCampaignName.com

betterschools@YourCampaignName.com

B E T T E R   S C H O O L S

Committee to Elect Brown—Pete Smith, Treasurer

---

sheets, using a computer-generated letterhead is cheaper than printing. If your computer consultant has a color printer, a two-color letterhead can be used to enhance your message. The format could be something like this: On the top you have the basic information; do your campaign theme in color, using an eye-catching font. At the bottom, in tiny letters, the election law disclosure information should be included, if required. But always include the committee name so people will know to whom to make out contribution checks.

Name Tags.

In another part of this book, I recommend using name tags to enhance name identification. You can buy them, but another simple but useful task for your computer is to print up a bunch of those name tags, which can be worn by volunteers when they go door to door and even by the candidate himself. Office supply stores have blank adhesive mailing labels, usually in color. A box of 500 or 1,000 is only a few dollars, and you can print up a very attractive name tag. Things get hectic in October and more so as the November election day approaches; if, in July, you run off a thousand name tags, they will be there when you need them in October.

The fact that name tags can be printed up weeks or even months in advance of the election demonstrates a point about how computers should be used. Electioneering is a people thing; staring at flashing images on a monitor is not. Computers are most effective in the planning and preparation stages of a campaign; when it's time to hit the streets, the computer's work should have already been completed.

Calendar and Scheduling.

There are several scheduling programs for computers that are pretty good. Having a big calendar posted on the wall at the campaign headquarters with all the dates listed is a necessity. A calendar there for everyone to see gives people a sense of how things are going and what needs to be done. You may want to have a separate computer schedule, however, especially one that gives you prompts for deadlines. With some programs you can type in a date and an event or a thing to do far in the future; then, on that date, the computer will remind you of that event. The computer person can keep a schedule on a computer as a backup to ensure that things get done on time.

Maps.

Maps are important in a local race. As with the calendar, I recommend that a large map of the candidate's electoral district be prepared and hung on the wall at the headquarters. This map is available to all and a handy, ready reference for volunteers.

Specialized maps, however, can help in achieving some tasks and in making your volunteers more efficient. In another chapter I discuss the strategy of having one volunteer in each precinct and winning your race one precinct at a time. The precinct volunteer may know the neighborhood, but having an exact map of the entire precinct helps. It sets definite boundaries and lets volunteers know exactly where they must work.

Computer map programs can be used to prepare these maps. Delorme has a program called Street Atlas USA, which has virtually every street in the United States on one CD. This is not the only street program, of course, but I am impressed with its detail. It will produce a map down to a scale of one inch equals 500 feet and will even indicate the range of house numbers on any given block, such as State St. 380 to 506. Free maps are also available over the Internet from mapquest.com and maps.google.com.

Such a detailed map would be very helpful to the volunteer. For example, suppose you want to get yard signs up the last week in September. You drop off the yard signs at the volunteer's house along with a precinct map and ask her to mark the location of each sign on the map. It is an easy way for the volunteer, and the volunteer coordinator, to see where and how many signs you have up in that precinct. It is also a control to be used for removing the signs after the election.

For volunteers who are going door to door, a map of the area can be used in conjunction with a walking list to simplify the job. It also can be used as a control sheet where, as each street or part of a block is done, it is marked off on the map.

This may seem like a lot of work, and I suppose it is, but with a good computer setup all of this can be done long before election day and stored in the computer to be ready to use. I want to emphasize this point. Your headquarters computer will be used every day right up until election day. Your high-tech computer will be used long before that. As a matter of fact, all the things you will need a high-tech computer for ought to be finished at least six weeks before election day.

During the early part of a campaign, time goes dreadfully slow. If you have just won the primary in June, you are up and ready for battle, but nobody else really gives a damn about the November election in June. Use this time with your computer consultant to plan, prepare, print, and save all you have done on your computer. Come October—and it comes awfully fast—all your maps, cards, forms, and instruction sheets will be there waiting for you on the hard drive to call up on demand.

Brochure.

Computer graphics are a real boon to the small campaign. When preparing your candidate's brochure, you can produce half a dozen sample brochures using different styles, formats, and fonts, and then pick the one that seems most effective. Don't go mad with computer design of the brochure; keep it simple. Have your computer consultant read the chapter about campaign literature first, and then begin designing.

Most computer people have a graphics program that can be used to add drawings, symbols, and designs in your brochure. Microsoft Publisher is a good, inexpensive, easy-to-use program. Scanners, which basically are copy machines that copy material into your computer instead of on paper, can be used to integrate some local recognizable symbol into your brochure. With a color printer, you can try various color schemes. One real advantage to this is that it gives you a first-hand look at what your brochure will be like if you use one, two, or maybe even three colors. When getting estimates from the print shop, you can get price quotes on the three different styles of the brochure and decide if having additional colors is worth the extra cost. You can do the same thing in trying to design an effective and readable yard sign. See what it looks like on the computer first.

Voter Lists.

Computerized lists of registered voters are readily available, but these lists have to be modified to suit your particular needs. This is where your computer consultant can really prove his worth. Some lists contain only the basic name, address, and party affiliation. Others contain additional information such as age or occupation, and some have even the voting history of the registrant. This additional data can be very useful to target your mailing or door-to-door efforts, but it has to be sorted out and put into a workable format.

Most raw voter lists are prepared by the elections office using an ASCII tab, DBS, SDF format, or something similar. This data can be transferred into your database program and, once in that format, is easily manipulated to make up almost any kind of list you want. I don't know how it's done, but I know computer people who tell me it is no big thing, given a reasonably powerful computer and a good database program. One of the tasks for your computer consultant will be to convert your voter's list into a database format and to use the database to produce the kinds of other lists you want. The accompanying CD-ROM contains an example that manipulates a full year's worth of election data for a state to show what is possible.

Let me give you an example of how you can use a computer to simplify a campaign procedure. Suppose you are running in a Republican primary and want to go door to door and talk to all the registered Republicans on Sunnyside Street. The easiest way to do this is to walk down one side of the street, skipping all the houses with Democrats, Independents, or non-voters, and then come back on the other side doing the same thing. If you have a computerized list of registered voters, you can have the names on Sunnyside arranged by house number going from the lowest odd number to the highest odd number, and then from the highest even number back down to the lowest even number. You then instruct the computer to eliminate all names that don't have an "R"—and voila—it prints out a list of exactly which houses to go to and in the right order. This is called a walking list, and you can see how helpful it would be in door-to-door campaigning. Some states sell walking lists, but doing your own is cheaper.

A walking list is only one example, and I am not saying you should get a walking list per se, but rather that you should think, plan, and talk with your computer expert about ways the computer can make your campaign more efficient.

Further on in this book is a chapter about getting a good mailing list and doing an effective mailing. Have your computer consultant read those chapters. If you are going to do a mailing, the computer consultant can not only save postage by targeting the names you want to reach, he or she can use a bar-coding software program to get the maximum bulk mail discounts.

In closing, let us emphasize how important it is to start working with your computer consultant early. It is easy to write about how simple it is for a computer to do this or that, but the many things I have suggested take time and effort. Not only that, they must be done long before the election. If the election is November 3, the computer consultant will have had to have done the following by Labor Day:

1. Get a headquarters computer and printer.
2. Have all the forms, letterhead, instruction sheets, and so forth set up and available by menu on the headquarters computer.
3. Have maps and walking lists prepared for each precinct.
4. Have a voter list transferred into database format.

5. Prepare a mailing list and obtain CASS certification.

6. Save everything on backup disks.

This is a lot of work, so be sure the computer consultant is involved in the very earliest stage of planning and preparation so the work can be done and saved ahead of time.

Speaking of saving stuff, save everything on disks. You will need some of the lists immediately after the campaign for sending thank you notes and so on, but when I say save everything, I am thinking about the next election. So should you. There is a good chance you will win, and an even better chance you will want to run for reelection. Two or four years from now may seem a long way off, but if you have all the names, all the lists, and all the instructions and forms saved on computer disks, then the next time out you will be ready to go with just a little bit of updating.

One final point, perhaps a philosophical one, should be made here. Your campaign computer system depends on your ability to pick the right person and to rely on what he or she does. This is the same kind of problem you will face in office—how to pick good people. Using a computer in your campaign is only partly a matter of getting the right software and the right hardware; ultimately, it is a question of how good your computer person is. So pick a good one.

PART II

CAMPAIGNING: THE PEOPLE

The first part of this book dealt with planning the campaign, with doing all the things necessary to get on the ballot and prepare for your race. Planning is critical, but as the Scottish poet Robert Burns said, "The best laid schemes o' mice an' men gang aft a-gley."

If you plan to win an election, you will need people. This is the people part of the book that talks about all the people involved from the candidate to the precinct volunteer. These are the people who will help you to win, the people who will carry out the plans you have made. This part of the book talks about how to get those people, and how you can use them most effectively to carry out your plan for winning.

We have a chapter devoted to two of the most important people in your campaign, the campaign manager and the volunteer coordinator. Have them read the chapter that describes their duties. This will not only give them a good idea of how important their responsibilities are but also will assist them in accomplishing those tasks.

We also have a chapter on that most important person of all, the candidate. If you have never been a candidate or have never run for public office before, you probably have some anxiety. Most first-time candidates have questions about what a candidate should do or how a candidate should act. We have some suggestions for the candidate on fundamentals of campaigning and the basic do's and don'ts.

It may seem odd that we included the chapter on money and fund-raising in the people section, but fund-raising is entirely a people kind of thing. It is the person-to-person contact that raises funds, and it is your people—your friends and volunteers—who will carry the ball on fund-raising. Fund-raising is hard, but the more people you have working at it, the more successful it is likely to be. We have some ideas for successful fund-raising and how to do it.

We finish this part of the book with a chapter that talks about only one person, the precinct volunteer. Everyone knows about the importance of having the right person in the right place at the right time. In your race, the right person is the precinct volunteer, the right place is in each precinct that you must carry in order to win, and the right time is in the weeks before election day.

James Reston, a columnist for the *New York Times*, once said that politics in America is like a pick-up game of baseball. The captain asks the people who he thinks will help win to join his team. If he is good at picking, and puts the right people in the right place, the team will win.

This is a good analogy. If you pick the right people, you will win.

→ 10 ←

YOU HAVE
TO HAVE A PLAN

If wishes were horses, beggars would ride.

—My mother

I must have spent a great part of my childhood wishing for things, because that was one of my mother's favorite expressions. She said it over and over again, and as a general rule, motherly advice is good advice—wishful thinking doesn't get you anywhere. But in planning a political campaign, a little wishful thinking at the planning stage can be helpful.

What you wish to do is to run a perfect campaign—one where everything goes exactly according to plan, and you win. The first step in planning is thinking about the way you would like it to go.

Imagine that it is a few weeks after the election and someone asks you what you did to win the race. You would tell him that you started out on such and such a day and did this, and then this, and so on. After the election is over, you will have a history of the campaign. Planning is writing that history ahead of time. In a well-organized campaign, the plan and the history will be remarkably similar. The difference between wishing and planning is that planning is what makes it go the way you wish it to go.

In Appendix C, there is a planning form. It is a chronological list of things to do based on a schedule beginning eighteen weeks before the election. You can use that form to plan your campaign, although you will have to alter it somewhat to fit the particularities of your race.

Before you file for an office, you have time to sit down and think about what it is you and your people will have to do if you are going to win. Having a prepared plan is a way of seeing that those things get done. During a campaign, when things get hectic, having the plan gives you a sense of direction and control.

Below is a list of things that ought to be included in creating your campaign plan. It is, like the form in Appendix C, based on an eighteen-week schedule. Since politics does not exist in a vacuum, we have chosen a sample race as an example—a race for the school board where there is no primary.

Your election will probably be different from this sample, but the basic principles are the same. For example, our sample election presumes a petition filing date 75 days before the election and the opening of a headquarters after the filing. If your petition filing deadline is closer to election day, you might find it advisable to plan to open the headquarters before the filing date. All campaigns are the same in that they require a plan, but each plan is different. So with those potential variations in mind, look at the following campaign plan as we count down to election day. As you read, try to think about how each item would apply in your race, and how it should be applied to your special situation.

Week Eighteen
Pick the office you want to run for.
Talk to your family and others.
Review your qualifications.
Contact local party officials.
Get petitions from board of elections.
Get financial reporting information and forms.
Send out news release saying you will run.

Start campaign calendar.

Do election statistics analysis.

Week Seventeen

Talk to the old hand.

Select a campaign manager.

Select a campaign treasurer.

Select a volunteer coordinator.

Hold first campaign staff meeting.

Start computer databases or written lists of contributors, volunteers, media addresses, etc.

Get maps of district.

Do demographic analysis.

Week Sixteen

Volunteer coordinator prepares petition-signing instructions for circulators.

Volunteer coordinator gets petitions out to be signed.

See what issues people are concerned about.

Have old hand review election statistics.

Week Fifteen

Second staff meeting—initial budget planning.

Estimate all internal campaign expenses such as rent, telephones, postage, stationery, copies, etc.

Estimate cost of the alternative campaigning methods such as radio, TV, bulk mail, first-class mail.

Estimate cost of printing literature, signs, etc.

Estimate revenue sources such as how much the candidate is willing to spend.

Consider other revenue sources, donations, fund-raisers, PAC money.

Do not try to resolve all budget questions at this time, but buy cable and radio time as early as possible to get the best spots.

Week Fourteen

Review statistics with staff and old hand.

Analyze each precinct and how many votes you can expect out of it.

Assign each precinct a priority in terms of how well you can expect to do there.

Pick your target number.

Start looking for speaking opportunities for the candidate.

Week Thirteen

Third staff meeting—issue analysis.

Talk to the old hand.

Rank issues in terms of importance.

Formulate candidate's position on each issue.

Select the most important issue—your issue.

Prepare a written statement of the candidate's position on that issue.

Choose a campaign theme. Coin a campaign slogan.

Week Twelve

Volunteer coordinator reports on how petition signing is going.

Prepare and design the basic campaign brochure with candidate's positions and qualifications.

Get mailing permit so number can be printed on the brochure.

Prepare the campaign forms to be used in headquarters—volunteer card, scheduler forms, precinct volunteer packets.

Start lining up the things needed for the campaign headquarters—telephone, desk, computer, copier, office supplies, stationery, stamps, etc.

Week Eleven

Start getting the signed petitions back from the circulators.

Check petitions for errors, compliance with the law.

Write the candidate's basic speech incorporating the campaign theme.

Locate a place to be the campaign headquarters.

Buy cable time; this must be done early to get good spots.

Week Ten

Final check of nominating petitions.

File your nominating petitions.

Open campaign checking account; open file for financial reporting requirements. Send out news release on your issue.

Print campaign brochure.

Week Nine

Check your opponent's nominating petitions to see if they can be invalidated.

Send thank you note to everyone who signed your petition along with a volunteer card and a ticket to your initial fund-raiser.

Week Eight

Open the headquarters—send out a news release. Invite all volunteers.

Post district map and campaign calendar in headquarters, and have all the campaign forms ready.

Hold your initial fund-raiser—send out news release.

Get computerized voter/mailing list.

Week Seven

Fourth staff meeting—budget planning.

Buy radio time—draft radio spots.

Candidate attends public meeting of office he intends to run for.

Send out news release.

Begin culling names to make up good mailing list.

Start hand addressing—get packets to volunteers.

Candidate event.

Get yard signs printed.

Week Six

Weekly staff meeting.

Enlist volunteers to write friends for donations.

Have coffee with voters at a west side location.
Cull computerized voter list.
Candidate event.
Candidate starts going door to door.

Week Five

Weekly staff meeting.
Produce radio spots.
Check on address packet volunteers.
Buy newspaper space.
Have coffee with voters at an east side location.
Candidate event.
Candidate continues going door to door.

Week Four

Weekly staff meeting—review budget and set final priorities.
Revise scheduling priorities, if need be.
Candidate goes door to door in Precincts A and B with volunteer.
Candidate event.
Get applications for absentee ballots.
Have coffee with voters at a north side location.
Start getting addressed envelopes back.
Volunteers to write to friends for votes.
Start putting up yard signs.

Week Three

Weekly staff meeting. Invite all volunteers.
Start radio spots—one per day.
Candidate goes door to door in Precincts C and D with volunteer.
Candidate event: League of Women Voters debate.
Candidate event.
First newspaper ads.
Push the addressers for their packets.

Week Two

Weekly staff meeting.

Radio spots—two per day.

Start sorting and bundling for bulk mail.

Have coffee with voters at a south side location.

Candidate goes door to door in Precincts E and F with volunteer.

Candidate event.

Candidate rest day.

Candidate event.

Second newspaper ads.

Cable spots—two per day.

Week One

Weekly staff meeting.

Mail first part of bulk mailing.

Radio spots—five per day.

Candidate event.

Candidate event.

Mail second part of bulk mailing.

Candidate goes door to door in Precincts G, H, and I with volunteer.

Candidate event.

Schedule volunteers to work polls handing out literature.

Cable spots—five per day.

Day One—Election Day

Vote.

Line up drivers to take people to polls.

Schedule volunteers to work polls handing out literature.

Day One Plus One—Victory Party!

This may seem like a long and involved plan, but actually it is quite short. Virtually all these events and things to do will happen in your campaign, and if you think reading about them is overwhelming, imagine what it will be like when they are actually happening and you are not prepared to deal with them because you have not planned for them.

Not everything will go according to plan. Unexpected events can really upset a campaign. But having a plan, having a set program you can turn to no matter what contingency arises, will help you bring order out of that chaos we call the democratic process.

THE SMALL CAMPAIGN

One final point should be made about campaign planning. We have directed this book toward the medium-sized campaign. The following chapters will suggest getting a campaign manager, finance chairman, scheduler, volunteer coordinator, and precinct volunteer in each precinct. That is like a small army, and you may be thinking that in your race, you will not need a huge staff. Perhaps. You may not need a separate person for each function, but do not lose sight of the fact that duties and functions of each of these positions have to be performed.

We talk about the "two hat" rule in Chapter 12, "The Campaign Manager," and strongly recommend that even in the smallest race every candidate have a campaign manager. You can double up on some of the other positions. One person can serve as scheduler and volunteer coordinator, and maybe even handle the financial reporting on the side.

You can do it this way, but we don't recommend it. First of all, this is how mistakes are made and why things do not get done. Many hands really do make the work light. A second reason is that the more people you have involved in your campaign, the better perspective it gives you. Staff people have ideas on how the candidate can be more effective, and they are more objective on how the campaign is going.

Politics is the art of inclusion, and the more people you include in your campaign, the more intimately you involve them in your race, the more likely it is you will run a successful race. When a person commits to any action on your behalf, it usually means that you get not only his or her vote but also the votes of the people they influence.

If you have a woman helping in your race, her husband, mother, father, mother-in-law, father-in-law, siblings, neighbors, coworkers, and friends are likely to think well of you because she is working for you and they respect her. The more committed she seems to be, the greater her participation and efforts on your behalf, the more likely these people are to think, "This candidate must be good, if Cecilia is working so hard for her."

This applies to all the people who might work for you. Therefore, it is important that you involve as many people as possible, and it is vital that you have specific tasks for them to do. It is an ironic reality of the small campaign, but the more favors you ask of people, the more willing they are to do them. The more favors you get from them, the more successful your campaign will be.

In any event, the need to make a plan and follow that plan is absolutely crucial, whether it is a big race or a small one.

→ 11 ←

Scheduling

and a Calendar

Time is what we want most, but alas, what we use worst.
—William Penn

Procrastination is the art of keeping up with yesterday.
—Don Marquis

You might think that it is easier to run for local office than to run for senator or president. After all, running for those big-time offices is so completely time consuming, the candidates have to work at it day and night. Don't kid yourself. Your campaign is going to be just as time consuming. You are going to be working just as hard, and the only real difference between you and a guy running in a statewide race is the distance between campaign stops. As a matter of fact, a candidate for the Senate usually has a staff of aides to help with the details so he can work at it full-time. You, on the other hand, probably have job and family responsibilities but no minions to do your bidding, so you have a greater need to budget your time.

On the day you decide, definitely, to run for office, make up a campaign calendar. It should be large enough to be seen when posted on a wall. There should be a block for each day until election day, and each block needs plenty of space to write in things to be done. Sometimes you can find large desk pads printed out like this, but if not, just make up your own calendar. This calendar will be posted in your headquarters and will be used to schedule all events.

Begin by writing the filing deadlines in on the calendar. There are tasks in a campaign that are required to be done by a certain date, such as the day on which you have to file your nominating petitions, or declaration of candidacy, in order to get on the ballot. This may be weeks or even months before the actual election. For example, in South Dakota the filing deadline is eight weeks, so to be on the ballot for the June 6, 2006, primary, a candidate had to file no later than April 4, 2006. In Ohio, for the May 2, 2006, primary, the filing deadline was February 18, 2006, seventy-five days—almost eleven weeks—before the primary and a full 260 days before the general election in November.

The actual date for doing these mandatory tasks will vary depending on your state's election laws. The requirement that they be done on time does not vary. The supreme court in virtually every state has held that candidates must strictly comply with all time requirements. All these judicial decisions are written in overblown language of the law, speak of weighty Constitutional principles, and talk about judicial restraint. Judges can tell you that these cases really come down to three reasons why the courts insist that the elections law be strictly followed. Stripped of the legalese, the judges look at the case of a candidate who has not filed on time or who has violated some regulation and say:

1. We don't want to get involved. We don't want to have to take sides in this political dispute. Case dismissed!
2. We don't get paid for piecework. If we allow this exception, we will get more cases like this. If we insist on strict compliance, we will get fewer cases. Case dismissed!
3. This guy is a jerk. If he can't follow the election law, what kind of elected official will he make? Case dismissed!

The rule of law for all states requiring compliance with time deadlines is: If you don't, you're out. It is as simple as that.

This is why we told you to get a copy of the brochure on your local election laws. Using that brochure, find the actual deadline dates as they apply to your election and make a list, like the one below.

August 3—Petition filing deadline
August 23—Designation of campaign treasurer
August 31—Preprimary financial report
September 14—Primary election day
September 28—Postprimary financial report
October 15—Preelection financial report
November 2—Election day
December 2—Final financial report

Start with the first deadline (e.g., the petition filing day), and in the box for that date on the campaign calendar write in large red letters PETITION FILING DEADLINE. Then go to the next mandatory date (e.g., the date for filing the name of your campaign treasurer), and write that date in, again in bright red letters. Do this for every other required date, even if you think that deadline will not apply to your race.

Once you have the actual deadline dates entered, count back an appropriate number of days and put in the tickler dates. These are the dates to remind people of the upcoming deadline. If the finance report is due August 31, then the August 24 box ought to have something like CHECK WITH JANIS ABOUT FIN. REPT.

If you wonder if all this is really necessary, just keep in mind that the law books are full of cases of candidates who missed a deadline and who, as we said before, always lose. This is the don't-blow-it part of our advice—telling you how to set up a calendar to avoid mistakes.

There is another, more practical reason for setting up the calendar. It makes for a far more efficient campaign.

In Chapter 10, we emphasized the need for a plan, a list of everything that will have to be done. This is what the scheduler does—fills in the actual date for every event, task, duty, and item mentioned in the plan.

This is why the scheduler is so important. If you have done as we have said, at this stage you will have a large, almost empty calendar. You will have the deadline dates filled in, but the rest of the dates will just be empty boxes. The scheduler's job is to fill in those boxes.

Keep in mind that we said the calendar should be made up on the day you definitely decide to run. This may be well in advance of filing day and months before election day, but you have to plan this far in advance. Using the example we provided, if August 3 is the petition filing deadline, that means all the petitions should be back in the headquarters no later than July 27, so they can be checked to be sure they are valid and there are enough names. You will need time to get more names if you're short.

The petition circulators are going to need some time to get the signatures, so if the petitions are due back July 27, the blank petitions have to be sent to the circulators on June 27. If you are going to prepare an instruction sheet for circulators (see the sample in the appendix), that has to be done before June 27. The scheduler should put on the calendar the start dates, the "check to see if it is being done" dates, and the target completion dates.

For example, if you are going to do a mailing in October, then you have to have a date for getting the bulk mail permit from the post office, a date for getting the material to the printer, a date for getting the mailing lists, a date to get the stuff out to be addressed, and then a date to get it back so it can be sorted by zip code. If you don't start thinking about the mailing until September, you are likely to do a very bad job of it or not be able to do it at all.

Keep in mind that in July, very few voters are really interested in the election in November. It is hard to campaign then, but you can work by doing some organizational things so that, come September, everything is in place and you're ready to take your message to the voters. You may want to use blocks of time, and schedule your own deadlines. For example, you may block all September for addressing envelopes and set October 1 as the deadline, so the volunteers can concentrate on addressing in September and going door to door in October.

After adding the planning dates, your campaign calendar will begin to look a bit more filled in. There will be dates for many things to be done long before election day. The first part of the calendar will be filled up, but the part closer to election day will still be relatively blank. This is the second part of the scheduler's job—scheduling the candidate's time.

After putting in all the planning dates, the scheduler should start putting in the must-be-there appearances for the candidate. In every local election there are certain events that the candidate should attend because they are such a great opportunity to meet with voters. It might be the festival at St. Teresa's Church, the rodeo, the JayCees pancake breakfast, the NAACP annual dinner, or the political party's dinner. There are events that get good media coverage or target voters, like a League of Women Voters Meet the Candidates Night. There will be at least one fund-raising event.

The scheduler's job is to see to it that the candidate gets to all these priority events and that they are listed on the calendar as priority events. Then, the scheduler puts in the events with a lesser priority, like a coffee at a volunteer's house. Then, the scheduler finds events or something for the candidate to do when there is an open date.

In Appendix F, we have a sample scheduling form. These forms should be used to find places and events where the candidate can meet with and talk to voters. These forms should be passed out to every volunteer. When the candidate gets a request to speak from some organization, the information should be written down on one of the scheduling forms. The scheduler should look for events where the candidate can show up and meet people. Every event should be marked on the calendar, even if there are conflicts.

Let's take the example of September 28, which we used previously, as a date for a filing deadline. When we started out, the September 28 box looked like this:

```
Sept. 28
    POSTPRIMARY FINANCE REPORT DUE!
```

If the scheduler has done the job well, and as the parts of the plan are integrated and carried out, then as September 28 approaches, the box ought to look something like this:

```
Sept. 28
    POSTPRIMARY FINANCE REPORT DUE!
    Weekly staff meeting
    Coffee at Shelia Eirmann's 6:00 p.m.
    NAACP dinner, Morton Hall, 7:30 p.m.
    Envelopes Ward A, to be returned, check w/
        Grace
    Send out news release on zoning changes
```

This is how you win. Things on the calendar will get done. The report will be filed. The staff meeting will be rescheduled. There will be a driver at Eirmann's at 7:15 so the candidate can be on time for the dinner and not have to hunt for a parking place. Since the envelopes for Ward A are all addressed, Grace can get the volunteers started on doing the addresses in Ward B.

The scheduler's job is not to see that everything is done. Various people have various responsibilities. The scheduler's job, though, is to see to it that everything that has to be done is written down on the calendar. If it is not written in on the calendar, it may not get done. This is how you lose.

Even if it is written down, however, it still may not get done. This is why the campaign manager, the subject of the next chapter, is so important.

→ 12 ←

THE CAMPAIGN MANAGER

I only have two hands!

> —Your Mother

I get by with a little help from my friends.

> —The Beatles

No child in America ever grows to adulthood without his or her mother, in a moment of frustration with all the demands on her, pointing out that the number of her hands is limited to two. As a candidate, you are going to feel that kind of pressure and you are going to need a little help from your friends. First of all, you are going to need the help of a good campaign manager.

For example, in the chapter on scheduling, we said the scheduler's job is to see that everything gets put on the calendar. It is the campaign manager's job to see that everything scheduled gets done, done well, and on time. Think about the kind of person you will need to do that kind of job.

Movies starring Robert Redford are usually pretty good, and the movies he directs are also good. The movies where he is both star and director, however, are not really bad, but they are not very good either—just kind of mediocre. This is because Redford is violating the "two hat" rule. This rule does not say that a person cannot wear two hats but only that if he does, he is not likely to do either job very well.

Politics follows the "two hat" rule. One person wears the candidate hat and does candidate things. Another person wears the campaign manager hat and manages the campaign. Their relationship is sort of like the quarterback and the coach, who, even though they are on the football field at the same time, do quite different things. Out on the field, the quarterback acts, reacts, and responds immediately. The coach stands off at the sidelines and watches. He thinks, analyzes, and plans the overall game strategy.

The relationship between a candidate and his or her campaign manager should be like that. The candidate is out front meeting and talking to people and listening to them. He has a busy schedule of places to be and things to do. The campaign manager is doing the things behind the scenes that have to be done to assist the candidate. If the quarterback is going to try a sweep around the left side, the coach must send a couple of fast linemen in ahead of time to block for him. If the candidate is going to be shaking hands at a factory gate, the campaign manager ought to have a couple of volunteers with him to pass out literature. Football or politics, it's the same game. When the guy carrying the ball moves, someone has to see that the whole team is there moving with him. In your race, the campaign manager is the "someone."

In the previous chapters we talked about analyzing the election statistics, getting maps, working out an overall campaign theme, and so forth. We talked about getting a headquarters, a computer, and district and precinct maps. Who is going to do all this stuff? Not the candidate; he won't have the time. Besides, if he is going to win, he has to be out getting votes. Nonetheless, these things still have to be done and the candidate has to find a campaign manager who will see that they get done.

Who should you get to manage your campaign? Don't pick your spouse. A political campaign puts both spouses under a lot of pressure, because as the one spends more and more time campaigning, the family responsibilities fall on the other.

There are also a lot of campaign events where it is expected that both the candidate and spouse will attend, and having your spouse there with you can help reach more people in the crowd. On the other hand, some spouses hate campaigning and this is why we suggest talking it over before you file. Running for office often puts a strain on the marital relationship.

The main reason for recommending against your spouse as campaign manager is that we assume that you are in love with each other, and the plain truth is that people in love are not objective. The campaign manager has to be objective. He has to be able to view things with a cool head, particularly as the campaign heats up. He has to be able to criticize the candidate, to point out mistakes, and to candidly say who is at fault when things go wrong. And things will go wrong!

Pick a friend, someone whose judgment you trust. Choose someone who knows how to work with people, not merely one who knows how to get things done, but one who knows how to get other people to get things done. Make the selection early. Once you have decided to run, the next step, and a very crucial one, is to select the person who will be your campaign manager. If you can find someone who is able, in spite of all the surprises and distractions, to keep the campaign on schedule according to the original plan, it will be not only your first but also your best decision.

Since the campaign manager's job is primarily to keep the campaign running according to the original plan, he or she has to be in on the planning. As soon as the campaign manager has been chosen, the two of you have to start planning. From then on, everything that follows ought to be the result of a joint decision-making process. You and the campaign manager will talk to the old hand together, decide who to get to handle the finances, who would be a good volunteer coordinator, and where to get money.

We spent a whole chapter talking about how you have to have a plan, but frankly, having a plan is no good at all unless it is carried out. We talked about having a campaign calendar and scheduling events so that things get done on time. In the chapter on making a calendar, we showed how, by the time September 28 actually rolls around, the calendar might read something like this:

> Sept. 28
> POSTPRIMARY FINANCE REPORT DUE!
> Weekly staff meeting
> Coffee at Shelia Eirmann's 6:00 p.m.
> NAACP dinner, Morton Hall, 7:30 p.m.
> Envelopes Ward A, to be returned, check w/ Grace
> Send out news release on zoning changes

This is an awful lot of stuff to do in one day. But if one person, the campaign manager, can take care of the financial report, check on whether the envelopes got addressed as scheduled, and send out the news release, the other person, the candidate, can be out getting votes.

Generally speaking, most of the time the candidate spends at the headquarters is wasted. He already has the votes of all the people there. What he needs is to be out at the Eirmann house trying to raise a little money from the people there. He needs to be shaking hands and talking to the people at the NAACP dinner and, just as important, listening to them. But most of all, he needs to know that while he is out doing this, the campaign is still moving forward in his absence.

So, how does the campaign manager keep things moving forward? It is an oversimplification to say the scheduler's job is just to write things down on the calendar, while the campaign manager's job is to check them off as they are completed, but that comes very close to the truth. The campaign manager is involved in all of the aspects of planning—budgeting, research, the campaign theme, mailing, radio, fund-raising. Once the plan is decided upon, however, his duties shift from being a thinker to being a doer.

In Appendix C there is a campaign planning form much like the one we discussed in Chapter 10, which includes many of the events and things to do in every race. Have that sample form typed into a word processor, because using the Insert key, the Delete key, and the Move Copy key is the best way to tailor it to your campaign. Delete irrelevant items, add those things that are particular to your local race, and then move them around until they are in the order in which you will do them.

Almost all of these items will go on the headquarters calendar, but the campaign manager should have his own copy with the same information recorded and should keep it with him for handy reference. He follows the plan, and as things get done, he checks them off, in his book and on the calendar.

This sounds a bit complicated and maybe even cumbersome, but using this method goes a long way in simplifying the campaign manager's duties. He or she is charged with seeing that it all gets done, an overwhelming task, but if the campaign manager can work on getting things done one at a time, the task is made more workable.

The campaign manager should have a day book, a pocket calendar large enough to make entries and to add notes. The plan should be duplicated in that book, in ink, and when something comes up, it should be penciled in. Make notes. Things that get written down get done; things that you try to remember get forgotten.

The campaign manager conducts the regularly scheduled staff meetings. The candidate should be there, but if he has a conflict, the meeting should be held anyway. The staff meetings should be informal, and try to get as many people as possible at the staff meeting. A good campaign has a lot of people each doing a special task, but it helps if occasionally they all get together and discuss the overall campaign. It builds morale and gives the volunteers a sense of how important their individual job is to the whole campaign. Finally, the staff meeting can be a source of good ideas because two heads, or a dozen heads, are better than one.

The campaign manager is a juggler who keeps five or six balls in the air at one time. On any given day in a typical campaign, envelopes are being addressed, volunteers are going door to door, and fund-raising tickets are being sold—all at the same time. The campaign manager "manages" these separate tasks but, frankly, the verb "juggle" is far more appropriate because in a typical race, things get hectic.

Keep in mind that although the campaign manager is the top dog, he is also the bottom dog if need be. If you are short a person when you are going door to door, the campaign manager fills in. If you have six volunteers addressing envelopes at an addressing party at the headquarters, and the coffee runs out or the waste baskets need to be emptied, it is better to keep the volunteers at their addressing and have the campaign manager do it.

The campaign manager makes adjustments. Having a plan is a good idea, but in the words of Murphy's Law, the probability of any event is inversely proportional to its desirability; or, if things can go wrong, they will.

Slavish adherence to the plan when things are not going as planned is silly. The plan is like a sea route charted on a map. The captain tries to follow that route, but wind, tides, and storms continually carry the boat in other directions. A good skipper never loses sight of the planned route to the ultimate destination, but he is continually making course adjustments. A campaign manager does the same thing. If the money is not there for the mailing you planned to do in a certain area, you don't write that area off. The campaign manager starts thinking and asking about ways to reach those voters by alternative means. This is why it is important to get as many people as possible at the staff meetings. One of them might have an idea.

The campaign manager is a listener who not only listens to the volunteers but also tries to get a sense of the public mood in general. Polling or public opinion sampling is very expensive, too expensive to even be discussed in a book about local campaigning, but in every race the candidate would like to have a sense of how things are going.

The candidate, however, is the worst person to assess campaign status. While it is often said that candidates lie to the people, it is usually the other way around. Americans are usually polite, and rarely does a voter come up to a candidate and say, "I won't vote for you." Instead, they hold their tongues and smile politely, all the while thinking to themselves, "What a jerk!"

The campaign manager, however, can get a more realistic sense of the mood of the public. He should talk to local people, ask the volunteers what they have heard, or check with the gossips at the local tavern or coffee shop. Is the message getting through? Are the voters looking at this election in terms of your basic campaign theme? Are they outraged by something the candidate has said? Is there one issue where the voters clearly see a difference between the candidate and the opponent?

This is where having a campaign manager who is objective is critical. He has to hear what is really being said and not what he wants to hear. Equally important, he has to tell the candidate what any candidate does not want to hear.

The candidate and campaign manager have to talk to each other regularly, and frequently the campaign manager will be the bearer of bad tidings. If the candidate respects the judgment and objectivity of his campaign manager, these talks can be productive. If something is wrong, if something is not working, changes can be made and things can be fixed.

If the campaign manager senses, for example, that the candidate is not reaching the voters with his position on the environment but that affirmative action is a hot issue, the candidate should rearrange the emphasis of his speeches. This is not to say the candidate switches his position or gives up what he believes is important but rather that he realizes that in this urban district employment is a bigger concern of the voters than forests of the Pacific Northwest. If something is not working, the campaign manager has to say so.

These talks are also about what is working. The candidate needs to know that the administrative things are being done. When we talk about the need for the candidate to exude confidence, we mean that a candidate who knows he or she is on schedule and that the work is being done comes across to the voters that way. Voters want efficient, competent people, and if the candidate looks like that sort of person, he or she will get votes.

Don't forget that the campaign manager has to be kept informed by the candidate about how it is going at the meeting-the-public end. If the candidate is getting positive feedback when he says something that seems to really reach the people, he has to tell the campaign manager about that and the campaign manager has to see if that issue can be emphasized in the time remaining.

Finally, the campaign manager has to make life easy for the candidate. Campaigning is hard, and the petty details of life often make it more difficult. The campaign manager has to be kind of a factotum or a gofer to the candidate. If the candidate is the mother of three whose husband is often out of town, and the campaign manager can always come up with a good, reliable babysitter, it is just one more little detail she doesn't have to worry about. If the candidate has a driver, a designated driver, he can relax at the cocktail party fund-raiser, or maybe have time to hang around after a meeting to talk to some people and raise money or get volunteers. Whatever makes life easier for the candidate makes him or her a better candidate.

The hand-in-glove analogy exemplifies the candidate and the campaign manager. One outside, one inside, but both working together in a relationship that is close and warm.

GETTING A
VOLUNTEER COORDINATOR

The world is full of people; some willing to work, and the rest willing to let them.

—Robert Frost

During the American Revolution, the Iroquois tribes sided with the British and one British general called on the Indians for help. A Mohawk chief, called Hendrick by the English, showed up with two or three hundred of his soldiers and assessed the military situation. He then turned to the English general and said, "What are we here for? If we are here to fight, we are too few. If we are here to die, we are too many."

That should be the attitude of your volunteer coordinator. If you are going to win, you will always have too few volunteers, and if you are going to lose, you will have wasted the time of too many people. The coordinator's job is to be concerned about the troops, the volunteers. He is like the top sergeant, the one who, whatever the strategy, sees to it that things get done.

The coordinator's first task is recruiting the volunteers. Recruiting volunteers is not as difficult as you might expect. You will be amazed how often someone will come up to you and ask how he or she can help. When that happens, the first thing you should do is ask for a contribution, because raising money is the hardest thing to do. More often than not, they will say that they cannot afford to contribute but would still like to help out in some way.

When they say that, have a volunteer card ready. Look at the sample volunteer card in Appendix E. A volunteer card is simply a sheet of paper or a three-by-five card with the name, address, and telephone number of the volunteer on the top and a list of things that the volunteer can do to help out. The volunteer fills out the card and checks off those things that he or she is willing to do.

Preparing this volunteer card menu is an important duty of the coordinator and should be done at the start of the campaign. In drawing up the campaign plan you develop an overall strategy, and in doing that you have to figure out all the things you expect to do during the campaign. Then you have to prepare a list of things that will need the help of volunteers. Having a list of tasks is helpful for potential volunteers because they can look at the list and see the things that will fit their schedules and talents. A businessman who travels a lot can put up a yard sign without much effort. Nobody can do everything, but everybody can do something. A housewife with five young children may not be able to get out of the house much, but she can make some phone calls or address envelopes. Nancy Pelosi, a stay-at-home mother long before she ran for Congress, volunteered regularly.

The items on the volunteer card should be integrated with the overall campaign strategy, and your volunteer card should have a category for anything you may want to be done. If the candidate is relatively unknown, one of the tactics will be to promote the name identification of your candidate, and then to make sure people get to know more about him. The plan to achieve this name recognition might call for a combination of yard signs, mailings, informal meetings in homes, and going door to door.

If this is the strategy, your volunteer card might look something like this:

I WOULD LIKE TO HELP.
I CAN DONATE $ _____

I can't donate, but I can help. I will
1. ___ Put a sign in my yard.
2. ___ Address envelopes.
3. ___ Invite some neighbors over to meet the candidate at my house.
4. ___ Go door to door
    ___ in the afternoon.
    ___ in the evening.
    ___ on weekends.
5. ___ Other: _____

Let's take a short digression here to talk about that "other" category. Your card should list the things you will want the volunteers to do, but always put that "other" category on your volunteer card. Quite often a volunteer will offer to do something you have not thought about. A young woman showed up at my headquarters once and in the other category wrote in "Photography." She was a photojournalism major at the local college, and very good at it. During that campaign, we often accompanied our news releases with professional-looking photographs, which got a lot of play, and all this for just the cost of the film, paper, and chemicals. She was happy to do it because it would look good in her portfolio when she graduated and went looking for a job.

In another race, a lawyer was moving into a new office in September but still had three months left on his old lease. He let us use the old office right up until the election, and since he bought all new furniture, the old place was even furnished with desks, filing cabinets, and a typewriter! Always ask your volunteers, as President Kennedy asked, what they can do for their country.

Never turn a volunteer down. If they offer to do something that is not in your plan, try to redirect them to what you want to have done. Political campaigns draw out some weird people, but remember that it takes all kinds of people to make a world, and some people can surprise you.

In 1972, when I was running for county prosecutor, I shared a headquarters with the local McGovern for President people. There were some old-line Democrats involved in that race, but also a strange assembly of volunteers. I learned a thing or two from that campaign.

One volunteer, a long-haired hippie with a scraggly beard, seemed to be able to raise other volunteers on a moment's notice. If they needed five or ten people, he would go out and return with them shortly. When I mentioned to a woman helping me that I found this remarkable, she gave me an odd look and said, "Don't you see? He's gorgeous!" That had not occurred to me. Sure enough, I took a second look at his volunteers and saw they were all college women, and every now and then one would look at him and smile.

Another McGovernite, a pleasant matronly lady who talked incessantly, seemed flighty and disorganized, but they put her in charge of addressing and she was terrific. By organizing addressing parties, she got 1,500–2,000 envelopes addressed every night. McGovern lost very badly nationwide, and only carried two counties in Ohio, but that oddball collection of volunteers saw to it that he carried their county. A group of dedicated volunteers will make the difference in almost any election.

The rule on recruiting volunteers is that if anyone shows any interest at all, give him a volunteer card. The coordinator's job is to get the cards out to potential volunteers and back after they have checked off what they want to do. In order to organize the various things that people have promised to do so that the volunteers can be used most effectively, sort through the volunteer cards and make up a list of volunteers by category—yard sign people, coffee people, drivers, precinct volunteers, and so forth. Some people will be in more than one category, and the list is open-ended because as the campaign goes on there will be more volunteers.

The coordinator works with the campaign manager who sets the start times and deadlines for the tasks that will involve the volunteers. The coordinator lines up the people to do whatever has to be done. While the campaign manager sees to it that things are done, the coordinator sees to the doing of them.

A good coordinator smoothes out the wrinkles. For example, a lot of cities have zoning laws that prohibit yard signs until so many days before an election. On that day, whenever it is, the coordinator should have those signs up. That means getting the list of yard sign people, dividing it up among the drivers, and seeing to it that they deliver the signs and perhaps even put them up themselves.

The volunteer coordinator has to keep a sharp eye on the campaign calendar and work closely with the scheduler. As we said in the chapter about scheduling, you should have no empty days. If someone has volunteered for a coffee in her home, and there is an open day for the candidate, the coordinator will try to have it scheduled for that day. The coordinator's job is a lot of backing and filling, getting things done as they come due, according to the overall plan, but also handling unexpected things as they come up.

There are planned events such as when your candidate is scheduled to speak at a Meet the Candidates Night sponsored by the League of Women Voters. For planned events, the coordinator will have plenty of time to arrange to have some volunteers attend. At this kind of appearance, you want to be sure someone in the audience will ask a question on your basic campaign theme. The coordinator will have volunteers in the audience ready to pitch the candidate a slow, soft ball that the candidate can knock out of the park.

But there are unplanned events, too. Suppose, on a slow news day the local TV station thinks that your campaign about sewers that keep backing up might be a news story and sends out a reporter and cameraman. It would not hurt for the coordinator to have a group of people from the neighborhood standing around in the background looking distressed as your candidate is being interviewed.

The campaign manager has to be a management-type person, but the volunteer coordinator has to be a people person. He or she has to get a lot of work out of people who are not being paid and cannot be fired or ordered around. They are, after all, only volunteers! Some people will offer to do things they are not competent to handle, and some will promise to do something and then not do it. Or do it wrong.

The volunteer coordinator has to avoid bruising egos. He can never say to a volunteer, "We don't want you," but must tactfully direct some eager, but hopeless, volunteer into some task that he can handle. He has to be able to ask the people who have already done a lot to do even more.

If your campaign is going well, you will keep getting more and more people offering to help. You may have planned to pass out literature in two precincts but find you have enough volunteers to do three. These new people have to be integrated into the plan, and the coordinator has to come up with more street maps, literature, drivers, and so on. Sometimes a new volunteer may be better suited to a task, but the "old-timer" who has been with the campaign will resent his "job" being given to some Johnny-come-lately.

If the campaign is going badly, tempers fray, and personal resentments develop between the volunteers, the coordinator has to smooth out the troubled waters. Every campaign will have bad days. The coordinator has to prevent bad days from becoming disastrous days.

It is quite a job, isn't it? A good volunteer coordinator plans how the volunteers are to be used. He recruits the volunteers. He schedules their work. He assigns them to the tasks. He sees that those tasks get done. He is worth his weight in gold. Just as the candidate has to rely on his campaign manager, the campaign manager has to depend on his volunteer coordinator. One very important decision will be your selection of a volunteer coordinator.

There is one final task for the coordinator that has to be mentioned. A volunteer may be willing to work like a dog for no more than an occasional thank you, but you better come through with that thank you. The coordinator has to be sure that people know they are appreciated. He has to say thanks a thousand times during the campaign.

Keep a list of every volunteer and, win or lose, the candidate should send each one a thank you note. If these people have helped you, as a matter of simple courtesy you owe them a thank you. If you expect these people to help out in another race, you better be darned sure they know how much you appreciated their help in this one.

⤳ 14 ⤴

THE CANDIDATE

This above all: to thine own self be true,
And it must follow as the night the day
Thou canst not then be false to any man.
                              —*Hamlet*, Act 1, Scene 3
                              (Polonius's advice to Laertes)

If you are wondering about what kind of candidate you should be or how to go about campaigning, keep in mind that you are what you are. This book, nor much else for that matter, is not going to change the kind of person you are, so don't be concerned about creating an image or developing a campaign persona. The most important thing for you as a candidate is to be yourself.

There are a few general things that a candidate should be, and some things every candidate should do, so we are going to give you lists of them below.

THINGS A CANDIDATE SHOULD BE

Be Confident.

Before you filed your petitions, before you became a candidate, you looked at yourself and your qualifications and compared them to the duties of the office you are running for. Don't be afraid to point out your qualifications and how you can do the job.

Be Honest.

You are for certain things, and against others. You have some talents and abilities, and some drawbacks. Be open and straightforward with everybody. If you think you can lie, or even hedge, you are sadly mistaken. If you say you are for the new city income tax on the west side and say you are against it on the east side, those chickens will come home to roost. You might, as Lincoln said, fool some of the people some of the time, and get elected, but frankly it will be a job not worth having.

Be Polite.

Be polite to everybody, particularly your opponent. Every person you meet is a potential vote, and even at that, common decency says you ought to be polite. You will run into stupid people, arrogant people, and even obnoxious people, but they all vote, and in our democracy they have a right to have their own opinions.

Always be polite to your opponent. Sometimes this is very hard particularly in the heat of a campaign, but there are two very good reasons for doing so. One is philosophical. As a candidate you are not objective, and what you perceive as a personal attack may be a legitimate comment in opposition to what you propose. The other reason is far more practical—getting mad doesn't work. Being insulting or obnoxious to your opponent just doesn't get you any votes, even if you are responding in kind.

Be Informed—Be Informative.

Information is a two-way street, and in a political race perhaps it is a two-edged sword, which cuts both ways. The voters want the candidate to be informed—informed about the problems of that office, and particularly informed about their concerns. The voters also want to be told by the candidate about his qualifications, policies, plans for the office, and especially how he plans to deal with their particular concerns.

For example, if a candidate says, "I'm against the sewer rate increases," the people who are also against the increases may vote for him. If the candidate has done his homework, however, he would know that 30 percent of the district are people living on fixed incomes. If he says, "Many of the residents are pensioners, and these people just can't afford the new rates," the people will identify with the candidate as one who is informed and knows about them.

Being informative about yourself is the other edge of the sword. In the earlier chapters, we talked about studying such things as demographics, statistics, geography, and issues. During the campaign, all this work begins to pay benefits because it shows that you know the district and know the people in it.

People want to know something about the candidate, and they want a reason for voting for you. Tell them! Tell them why you are qualified by training or experience or both. If you are for a certain policy, tell them why you are for it! If you're against some other policy, tell them why it won't work or is too expensive. Tell them what you think.

Always be sure to have some of your candidate brochures with you ready to hand out to anyone who is interested. Some people will want to talk to you, but a lot of others will prefer to read about you, your qualifications, and positions.

Be on Time.

As a candidate, your time is precious, but don't start thinking it is more precious than the people who are waiting to see you. They have things to do, too. Being late is insulting and disrespectful, and you cannot get votes by showing people how little you think of them. Sometimes it happens that you are late, of course, and when it does, fall back on Rule 2—Be Honest—and Rule 3—Be Polite: apologize.

We could go on with things a good candidate should be, but it will begin to sound like the Boy Scout oath. "A Scout is trustworthy, loyal, helpful, friendly . . ." The purpose of the Boy Scout oath is to focus the scout's attention on those virtues. There is no candidate's oath like, "A candidate is confident, honest, polite, informative, punctual . . . ," but as a candidate you do have to keep all this in mind. If this conflicts with the "be yourself" advice, you are going to have a hard time winning.

THINGS A CANDIDATE SHOULD DO

There are a few things that a candidate ought to do to prepare before the campaigning actually begins.

Get a Candidate's Book.

When learning about the office and the district, you come across a lot of useful information such as statistics, budget figures, and so forth. A candidate should make up a little notebook of this useful information and have it with him at all times. If you get a very specific question, you can look it up. The voters do not expect you to know everything but are impressed with a candidate who has done his homework.

Get a Name Tag.

It does not have to be anything fancy. Office supply stores sell clip-on tags where you insert the name. Often you can cut your name out of one of your brochures and use that. You can buy rolls of adhesive lapel labels with your name printed on them. A good part of politics is name identification, and you want to make sure that people know who they are talking to. You want them to remember your name when they go to vote.

Prepare Your Basic Speech.

Often during the campaign, you will find that although you did not expect it, you are asked to get up and say a few words. This is where the campaign theme comes in. We said that you should decide on a statement of what you are for, your campaign theme. When given the chance to speak, even if you are not prepared, you can get up and give that basic statement of policy.

This should not be a memorized speech but more like the outline of a speech where you have all the topics lined up in an orderly fashion in your head. When asked to speak, you will be prepared to make your major points in an organized fashion.

You should have the basic speech not only in your head but also in the word processor. When you are called on to make a prepared speech, you can call it up and modify it to suit the occasion. We will talk more about that later.

Think about Getting a Driver.

A driver is not absolutely necessary, but if the district you are running in is large and it takes time to get from one campaign stop to another, it is handy to have someone to do the driving. Even in a small district in an urban area where the traffic is terrible, having a driver can be very helpful. With a driver, you arrive relaxed, you don't have to hunt for a parking space, and you are more likely to be on time. College kids, particularly political science majors, are often eager to be drivers as kind of an apprenticeship. A driver is not a necessity, but it is very good to have one, or even two so they can share the work. Talk to the volunteer coordinator about lining someone up for this.

CAMPAIGNING

Get Invited.

People are far more likely to vote for someone they have met. The more people you meet, the more people you talk to, the more votes you are going to get. So you have to get out and meet people. You have to get yourself invited to places where you can meet people, shake hands, or give a speech. Go to the county fair, the pancake breakfast, the festival, or wherever there is a chance to meet people.

Keep in mind that many events, by local custom, are nonpolitical. That is, people prefer that the candidates keep a low silhouette, or not even show up at all. Do not offend potential voters by violating the local rule. There are still a lot of places and groups that want to hear candidates. Find out which ones they are in your district and try to arrange a speaking engagement, or perhaps even a joint appearance with your opponent.

You will get a few invitations. For example, many local chapters of the League of Women Voters schedule Meet the Candidates Nights and invite all candidates to appear. If you wait around for invitations, however, you will lose out.

You will have to arrange a lot of your own speaking engagements. On the volunteer card, there is a space where the volunteer can arrange to have you speak to his or her group. Volunteers can hold coffees in their homes and give you a good opportunity to meet the neighborhood people and talk with them. You have to be a little pushy and get yourself invited to as many places as possible.

GIVING A SPEECH

We probably should have called this part "Talking to People" because everybody knows how to talk to people yet almost everybody is terrified of giving a speech. Think in terms of talking to people even when you are on a podium, looking out at several hundred people, as "giving a speech." Be relaxed, be yourself, and just tell them what you think. There are a few things to do to make the speech go easier.

Talk to This Audience.

First, speak to your audience's concern. When you prepare your talk, start with your basic speech but tailor it to suit that particular audience by adding material that is relevant to their problems. Statistics about population density and average residential occupancy might bore a general audience, but if you are addressing the Hough Heights Homeowners Association about zoning changes, these critical figures are interesting.

Be Brief.

Make your point in as few words as possible. Being brief is hard, particularly when dealing with complex issues like the long-term effects of toxins, for example. Nonetheless, when dealing with a complex issue you can bore people to death, and you are there to get votes. One real advantage to the basic speech is that when it is ended, you are finished.

Be Upbeat.

Do not whine and cry about the problems. Your audience knows what the problems are; they have come to hear your solutions. Be confident. Tell them how you are going to work on the solutions.

Take a High Tone.

Your opponent may be a sleazy, lying dog who is in cahoots with, and on the payroll of, every special interest group. If he is, let the voters find that out themselves. Tell them what you are about, what you are for. They don't want to hear your opinion of your opponent, and they will decide for themselves who is the better choice. They want to hear how you plan to carry out the duties of the office so they can make that choice.

Always Return to Your Theme.

In closing, always go back to your campaign theme. You have given your basic speech, you have added the details for this particular audience, and you want to leave them with that basic theme.

Always Ask for Questions.

If you are speaking to a very large group, asking for questions from the audience may not be practical, but for small groups it is almost always a good thing to do. First, it makes you look like someone who wants to hear from the people. Second, you might have inadvertently misspoke and created some confusion in your speech, and it is good to have that straightened out. Most important, it allows you to talk about what the audience is most concerned about.

QUESTIONS AND ANSWERS

The question-and-answer period is often fraught with pitfalls, so here are a few suggestions about Q and A.

Be Sure You Understand the Question.

When I was running for judge, an old man got up and with a heavy Southern accent asked, "What's your position on farms?" I was taken aback somewhat because judges do not make agricultural policy, so I told him I did not quite understand his question. He said, "Ya know, the ryat to bear ahrms, guns, fahrms." With his accent, "right" sounded like a two-syllable word and "firearm" was pronounced monosyllabically. Before you begin to answer, be sure you understand the question.

You Don't Need All the Votes.

In telling how to pick a target number, we said that you do not need all the votes, only 50 percent plus one. Remember that when answering questions. Do not try to tailor your answer to what you think the audience wants to hear. Be honest, and say exactly what you believe. No matter what answer you give, you will probably alienate some of the audience anyway, so just tell it like it is.

When you don't know the answer, say that you don't know. Don't try to fake an answer. You know bullcrap when you hear it, and you can be certain your audience does, too. You can hedge a bit, of course, and look it up in your candidate's book. Or you can say, "I haven't thought about that, but it is a good point and I am going to learn about it." Get the questioner's name and number and when you do find out about his concern, call him back or write a note and tell him your position on the issue. The voters cannot expect you to know everything, but they can expect you to be honest, and an honest "I don't know" may even get you a few votes.

THE CANDIDATE'S SANITY

Politics is a crazy, frustrating business, and the candidate has to maintain his or her sanity throughout the campaign. There are three things we recommend the candidate do to maintain a sense of balance.

Principle and Policy.

Remember the difference between questions of principle and questions of policy. Not everything is a matter of principle, and there can be legitimate policy differences about how to promote the principle. Both candidates might agree on the principle of equal opportunity but disagree on whether affirmative action is the best policy to achieve that goal. Every candidate for the school board is for good schools, but each candidate will have different ideas about what makes a school good.

Generally, political debate is not about issues of principle but issues of policy. Both sides of the gun-control issue agree on the principle of the right to personal safety, and the debate is really about which policy better promotes personal safety. When you campaign, remember that an attack on your policies is not a personal attack on you or your principles. When you attack, remember that your opponent has his principles, too, even if the policies he espouses are ignorant or wrongheaded.

Develop a Thick Skin.

A man who owns a newspaper in my district is from the other party and we do not like each other personally. In one race, his newspaper endorsed my opponent in glowing terms, as I expected, but their criticism of me was fairly tame. They said I was not very good at the job, but also said that sometimes I was not as bad as I usually was. All things considered, I did not think they were too hard on me, but my wife read the same editorial and she was outraged.

I have a thicker skin, perhaps because of the ruling by the U.S. Supreme Court in *New York Times v. Sullivan*, which is a leading case on libel. It said that everybody has the right to say anything they want about a public figure, and if you run for office, you are a public figure. What they say about you does not even have to be true; it can be completely false. It has to be both false and malicious to be libelous. Unless you can prove that they were motivated by actual malice, or are so careless with the truth that their carelessness amounted to malice, you cannot sue them. As a lawyer, I am telling you that is a very difficult burden of proof. You can sue, but you probably cannot win.

It is better to learn how to roll with the punches. People will call you names. The press will misquote you. You will get crank calls. There is this nasty side to local politics, and it sometimes seems that the smaller the electoral district, the dirtier the politics.

You have to remain above all this. If you don't, it will drive you crazy. Not only that, if you let them get to you, you may overreact and do something stupid. If you do, you may well lose. Always keep in mind that they would not bother to attack you unless you were winning, or close to winning. Be cool. Chill out. Keep your objective in mind, and do not dance like a puppet when they try to pull your string.

Get Some Rest.

For the candidate, the election contest is likely to be one of the most grueling experiences he or she has ever had. This whole book is directed toward telling you that you must work hard, but everybody needs a break.

In the movie *The Hustler*, Paul Newman plays Fast Eddie, the young challenger who takes on the preeminent pool shark Minnesota Fats, played by Jackie Gleason. They are playing eight ball and the game drags on for hours with neither player getting an advantage. Gleason asks to take a break and goes into the washroom. He washes his face. He washes his hands, and powders them with talc. He straightens his jacket and tie. Then, refreshed and renewed, he returns to the poolroom and beats the pants off Fast Eddie.

Every candidate needs to have a break like that. You will need a short respite, a day or perhaps even a weekend, where you can get away from the race. This rest should be scheduled on the campaign calendar, and you should resist the temptation to ignore it and keep working. If you take a break to do something you like to do, to spend a moment with your kids who are feeling neglected, to have a nice dinner with your spouse where the election is never mentioned, you will return to your race refreshed and with a better perspective.

Work as hard as you can, but be sure you maintain your sanity.

One final point should be made about being a candidate. You ought to be proud of what you are doing. Our democracy works because some people are willing to undertake the hardships of a political campaign and the rigors of managing the public's business.

Even if you win, you are not going to change the world, nor solve all its problems, and maybe you will not even accomplish most of what you had hoped to do in your elective office. But you will have run, and served, and tried to make things better. This is a noble calling and a worthwhile thing to do.

→ 15 ←

MONEY

AND FUND-RAISING

Money is the mother's milk of politics.

—Jesse Unruh,
former Speaker of the House, California

I feel qualified to write this book because I know a fair amount about many of the details of local campaigning, but in all honesty, if I were really good at political fund-raising, I would be chief justice of the state supreme court. What I can do, however, is tell you about some of the things I have learned about fund-raising and suggest some of the things you might want to try in your race.

The first thing to decide about fund-raising is whether you want to do it at all. Raising money is a demeaning sort of business. When I was running for the state supreme court, we got a $10,000 check in the mail from a labor PAC. They knew from the way I had decided cases in the past that I could be described as a friend of labor. No one had solicited that donation, no one said that the PAC expected me to vote a certain way on court cases, and as a matter of fact, nobody from that organization ever talked to me. Still I could not help but feel that they expected something for their money, and that if I did not realize that, I did not have enough sense to be on the state supreme court. My opponent in that race, Robert Holmes, who was the nicest guy I ever ran against, told me that whenever he got a large donation it made him feel the same way.

In a local campaign, you might decide to finance the race entirely out of your own pocket and not do any fund-raising at all. This can be very expensive; indeed, it is a luxury. Ross Perot, who is extremely rich, winced when he was told what a presidential campaign would cost. If you are in a smaller contest, however, and if you have a lot of volunteers, it is an alternative to consider.

When you finance your own campaign, you do not have to spend any time on fund-raising and can concentrate entirely on getting votes. It also simplifies the campaign financial reporting requirements since you have to list only one contributor. In some states, if the candidate spends only his own money and his expenses are below a certain level, he does not have to file a financial statement at all. Check this out by reading your local election regulations.

Paying it all out of your own pocket may not be possible, and even if the candidate is willing to spend a lot of his own money, most campaigns may have to resort to some kind of fund-raising to get the kind of money needed to win.

Fund-raising is hard! Mother Teresa, the selfless nun who won a Nobel Prize for her charitable work, said even she had a hard time raising money. There are many worthy endeavors putting the bite on people, and unfortunately most people do not think of politics as a worthy endeavor. If money is political mother's milk, the typical candidate feels like singing that old spiritual, "Sometimes I feel like a motherless child."

THE BUDGET

The first thing to do in planning the fund-raising for your race is work up a budget. You may think that you cannot prepare a budget until you know how much has been raised, but this is not the way to go about it. First you prepare a budget, and then you see about getting the money for each budget item. This is not unlike picking the target number of votes, but while it is quite easy to budget $1,000 for bulk mailing, it is very hard to get that thousand bucks. You have to design a budget based on different levels of anticipated income.

The budgeting process is one of setting priorities. The first step is to set what we shall call necessary costs, the costs of the basic campaign expenses, such as:

Headquarters rental
Phone
Stationery and envelopes
Office supplies
Postage
Printing candidate's brochure
Maps
Campaign and volunteer forms
Copier or computer costs

Since these are the basic necessities, they have to be given first priority. First, see what each of these items is likely to cost, then determine how you can supply each one without spending any money. You don't need to rent a headquarters if you can use somebody's rec room or a vacant storefront. Sometimes local parties have joint headquarters where you can have access to phones and office equipment. A volunteer might donate the use of a computer, and some computers have the graphics capacity with which to produce an adequate-looking letterhead, and sheets of return address labels, so you will not need to print stationery. These necessary expenses are basic but don't really get votes. Try to spend as little on them as possible.

Warning!

In most states, in-kind donations, such as the loan or use of property, must be reported as contributions. ↩

After you have worked out a budget for the necessary costs, there are what we call the discretionary costs. Generally, these discretionary costs involve a choice of alternatives, and how much you spend on them depends on the overall plan for the campaign. If your main campaign strategy is to do a bulk mailing, the costs for printing and postage are given first priority. You estimate the costs to do a complete mailing.

If there is additional money, you may want to buy radio ads, so these are given a second priority. Cable television, yard signs, billboards, and so on are each given a priority. Before you set the priority, try to estimate the amount of money it will cost to use each campaign technique effectively.

Preparing the budget then is just a matter of setting two columns—one on the cost, and the other on the source of the funds. The following figure (continued on page 128) gives a short sample.

NECESSARY COSTS

Necessity	*Cost*	*Source*
Headquarters rental	free	Joe's vacant store
Phone	$240.00	
Stationery, envelopes	80.00	
Office supplies	65.00	
Postage	58.00	
Printing candidate's brochure	465.00	
Maps	free	County engineer's office
Copier	free	Mary has one we can use
Computer	free	Phil's old one
Campaign and volunteer forms	free	Will prepare on computer
Total	**$908.00**	

DISCRETIONARY COSTS

Discretionary Item	Cost	Source
First Priority: Bulk mailing		
Printing	$0.065	
Postage	0.175	
Labels	0.015	
Total	**0.255**	
Cost to mail 3,200 pieces	$816.00	_____
Second Priority: Radio spots		
30-second spot WXYZ	$9.90	
Four spots per day	39.60	
Fifteen days	$594.00	_____
Third Priority: Cable television		
(And so on.)		

When you have a budget like this, fund-raising is just a matter of filling in the blanks. For each expense listed in the budget, you have to obtain a source of funds to pay that expense.

The important thing to remember is the priority given to each procedure. You may want to do a bulk mailing and radio, but what happens if you do not raise enough money to pay for both? You could do a little of each, but we do not recommend that. If your first priority is to do a mailing, do that and do it well. Spend all the money you get on the first-priority item and when you have completed that, then spend whatever is left on doing as much of the second as you can.

Using the budget as an example, a campaign may have raised $1,000. That money should be spent as follows:

$816—mailing
$184—radio

It is better to do one good mailing and follow up with some radio than to try to do half of each. You will only end up doing both badly. There is a very good reason why the English language is full of phrases like "half-cocked," "halfhearted," "half-baked," and the ever popular "half-assed."

Setting budget priorities and committing to the first priority is important because it sets targets for the fund-raising program and directs your activities toward specific goals. You may want to raise $4,000, or hope to raise $2,000, but it is absolutely necessary that you raise $1,000. Having a moderate sense of desperation is handy because fund-raising is so hard. If you are considering self-financing, you must have the budget and the priorities determined before you can make a reasonable decision about what the race will cost you.

When you have made up your budget, it is at this point you decide whether to pay for everything yourself or go the fund-raising route. Most candidates will have to take that second choice.

FUND-RAISING

Reduced to its simplest terms, fund-raising is cutting people loose from some of their money. There are all sorts of ways to do this, and what we suggest here are some that have worked fairly well in the past. You might have some ideas of your own and if you do, try them out.

Before we do, however, let's take a moment to talk about the kinds of fund-raising that do not work. General mail solicitations are expensive and almost never work. If a charity gets a 2 or 3 percent response to a solicitation letter, it is considered a success. If you write to someone and ask for a contribution and their vote, you might get the vote, but that's about all.

Do not expect any money from the local party even if you are the endorsed candidate. The local party will help you as much as it can. It will include you in its general mailings, invite you to the meetings where you can meet voters, make your literature available, but the simple fact is that most local parties don't have any money. The little they do have is spent on the candidates in general, getting the whole ticket elected, and no money is given to local candidates.

Another tactic that does not work is spending money to raise money. All fund-raising is net. The money spent trying to raise money is a dead loss. We will talk more about this when we discuss fund-raising events, but let's discuss some things that do work.

The Candidate's Request.

The most effective fund-raising technique in a local campaign is for the candidate to directly ask people for money. This cannot be a blind solicitation but must be made to people who are in some way familiar with the candidate.

Prepare a list of people for the candidate to contact—friends, relatives, business and professional associates, and so on. The candidate should contact each one and ask straight out for a donation. You will be amazed at how many people turn you down. Most will not refuse outright but promise to send a check and never do it. For those who do send a check, you will be somewhat amazed at how tight they are. You know this guy can easily afford fifty bucks and he sends a check for ten. Of course, no matter what the size of the donation, always send a thank you.

Always ask, though, because you will be surprised by the unlikely sources who contribute. We had a rebellious seventeen-year-old boy, who had been in a lot of trouble, working very hard as a volunteer in one campaign. His father showed up to drive him home (the son's driver's license had been suspended for DUI) and mentioned to the volunteer coordinator that the campaign seemed to have given the boy a sense of purpose. He was glad his son had found a cause he was interested in and willing to work for. She asked for a donation and he wrote out a check for $100 on the spot. Such is paternal gratitude. Always ask!

We generally recommend that neighborhood coffees be political events, a chance to meet and talk with voters. But you can use that same format as a fund-raiser, where instead of just talking about the issues the candidate asks the people there for money. Be sure the guests know before they are invited to that kind of coffee that they will be asked to contribute. But even at an ordinary coffee, if one of the attendees seems especially interested, have someone approach him and ask for a contribution.

Former Contributors.

Financial reporting laws require that the name and address of each contributor be listed, and these reports are usually filed with the local elections office or sometimes with the ethics office. These reports are public records and it may be well worth your time to look through reports filed in previous elections. See if you can find names of people you may want to contact for a contribution.

The Dedicated Gift.

This is an effective technique to use, particularly if you have made a good budget plan. If you have a supporter who you know is good for a donation, don't just ask for a contribution. He will probably send a check for less than you expect. Show him the budget and ask him if he can come up with the $80 to pay for the stationery. He may blanche at $80 and contribute $58 for the postage, but it is more than he might have given without being shown the budget. People want to know their money is being put to good use, and the dedicated gift does that.

Letters to Friends of Your Friends.

The candidate is not the only one who should be asking for money. Involve your friends and volunteers and ask them to try to raise contributions. One way is for each one to write a personal letter to five or six friends and ask for a donation. You can work in the dedicated gift idea here. Instead of just writing and asking for money, the writer explains how the campaign is going and says that you can buy one more radio ad or send out one hundred more pieces of mail if the friend would contribute $9.90 or $22.50.

Direct solicitation by the candidate or someone close to the campaign is effective, but there are other methods of fund-raising—the most common being some kind of fund-raising event.

The Fund-Raising Event.

To have a good fund-raiser there are a few things to do. You have to plan it, promote it, and sell tickets to it. All of which are easier said than done.

In planning any event, the cardinal rule is to keep it simple, and to keep the costs down. It does not do any good to sell $1,000 in tickets if it cost $900 to put on the event. As with everything else, see what can be donated and see what you can save by using your volunteers. If you can get someone to let you use their place for the event for free, and assure them that after it is over the volunteers will leave the place spotless, your net proceeds for the event will go up.

If you can get a contributor to underwrite the whole event, a variation on the dedicated gift theme, it is all clear profit. In one race in a city along the Ohio River, there was a paddle-wheel boat that could be rented for $200 per night. One contributor rented the boat, and they sold tickets at $10, $15 for a couple. A couple of volunteers brought jug wine, another a case of beer, and another brought some munchies and dip. There were no expenses, all the money was profit, and everyone had a nice time on the river.

Selling tickets to an event is hard. One method to use is the sell-five-tickets or buy-five-tickets plan. Everyone who is involved in the campaign is given five tickets with the understanding that they will either sell the five tickets or buy them themselves. For the people who hate to flog tickets to political events, it is often easier to buy the tickets themselves. If people buy tickets they are not going to use, be sure to get them back and pass them out to others, like student volunteers. It is always good to have a big crowd at a fund-raiser.

Another ploy is the nonevent fund-raiser; that is, a fund-raiser nobody goes to. Tickets are sold with the understanding that no one will attend. This appeals to people who are busy and are willing to buy tickets particularly if they don't have to attend.

Another good idea is to try to conduct a fifty/fifty raffle, sometimes called "split the pot," at any event you hold. The people in attendance are sold tickets for a dollar or two, and the winner gets half and the campaign gets half. As often as not, the winner will forego his or her half and donate it back to the campaign. On the boat trip mentioned, they did a fifty/fifty split, the winner refused his share, and they made another $67. In some states, this may be illegal, so be sure to check it out.

The kind of fund-raising event to hold depends on your locality and what your neighbors like to do. Fund-raisers are as varied as America itself. Try to have a fund-raiser that associates you with the district you are running in. It might be a polka party, a square dance, or a theater party, depending on where you live. Whatever it is, it should have a little bit of style. It should be the kind of event people want to go to.

There are spaghetti suppers, pancake breakfasts, and rib feasts, and each locality has many of these kinds of events for all sorts of causes, so try to make yours a little creative. There are a lot of chili suppers, but one I went to was very successful. It was promoted as a chili contest. Five people, four men and a woman, each claimed to make the best in the world and the fund-raiser was based on the idea that the attendees would vote on whose was best. Each contestant paid for his or her own ingredients, and it was held in a public park, so except for paper plates and cups and a few dollars for coffee and soft drinks, it was all profit. It was a great success, because each contestant brought along a claque to vote for his chili. (I would add as a parenthetical note that one of the chilies was tolerable, but the other four were just terrible. Good politics; bad indigestion.)

My wife organized a fund-raiser for a local charity. It was a "champagne and chocolate" party scheduled for St. Valentine's

Day. It was so successful that it has been repeated every year since, the only change being she got the local wine store and candy store to donate the goodies. Love, wine, and chocolate—something for everybody—and all net profit.

Having an interesting location can be an effective draw. In one town there was a big old historic mansion, which had been vacant for some years. A young couple moved into town, bought it, and began a restoration. They agreed to hold a cocktail party at the mansion, and the tickets sold like hotcakes. The candidate was not all that popular, but everyone wanted to see what they had done with the house. A boat, a garden, any kind of place that attracts people and makes them want to come, is a good setting for an event.

One group of women in a rural county raffled off a shotgun, while another women's group from a chichi suburb held an art auction. I have seen dart-throwing contests, bocce ball lessons, and muzzle-loading rifle turkey shoots all used successfully as fund-raising events. I could go on, but the point is: It should be fun, it should be cheap, it should be profitable.

Before we close on fund-raising events, we want to make one last point about the subject. Never lose sight of the objective. When the budget is prepared and the priorities established, the source of funds to pay for each priority is included in the budget. This is done to give your fund-raiser a specific goal. Using our sample budget, the first budget priority item is a mailing that will cost $816. That amount has to be the minimum net proceeds for your event. The boat ride was fun, and the chili was terrible, but it was the net profit from those events that made them successful. Your event may be very successful, or maybe not as successful as you hoped, but if you have a definite goal in mind, an exact dollar amount to strive for, you are much more likely to achieve that goal.

Fund-raising is hard, the hardest part of politics. When you make a budget, which sets your priorities, and then look for a source of funds to meet each priority, it is still hard, but you have made it more workable and achievable.

As an afterthought, we should mention the after-election fund-raiser. Contributors love winners, so a fund-raiser after you have won can be very successful. The proceeds can be used to pay off campaign debt, or as the start of a fund for the next election. These after-election fund-raisers are usually highly regulated, or even illegal in some places, so check your election laws first.

16

WINNING IT ONE PRECINCT AT A TIME

Inch by inch, and row by row, Oh, to make this garden grow.

—Anonymous folk song

The very first time I ran for office, I met a woman at a party function and we hit it off right away. We talked for a bit and she said to me, "Don't worry about my precinct. I'll see that you win there." I did win in her precinct, and although that precinct is about equally split between Democrats, Republicans, and Independents, in every subsequent election I carried that precinct by over 60 percent.

You might be thinking to yourself, "Gee, if I had a person like that in every precinct in my district, I would win hands down." Exactly! That is the whole point of this chapter. If you have one good, reliable worker in each precinct, you can win any election.

In the chapter on analyzing election statistics, we talked about picking your target number using a precinct-by-precinct analysis. We showed, in that example, how you could calculate your target number by determining that you needed 250 votes from Ward 5 Precinct A and 150 from Precinct B and so on. In your race, you will have to make that same kind of determination for each precinct. If you have a friend working for you in Precinct A, someone who will go out after that target number, you have a much better chance of winning there. If you have a friend or volunteer in every precinct, you can win in every precinct. The best campaign strategy for a local race, and the cheapest I might add, is to have a volunteer working for you in each precinct in your district. Finding so many volunteers may sound like a daunting task, but let's be objective about this. If you cannot find at least one person in the whole precinct who knows and likes you, your chances of winning are pretty slim anyway. Finding someone to be the precinct volunteer is really not all that hard.

The precinct volunteer should live in the precinct, or at least in the neighborhood. He or she should be somebody who knows the area and a little about the people who live there. The volunteer should be someone the other residents can identify with. If the precinct adjoins a large state university and is full of student apartments, get a student volunteer who lives in one of those apartments. But if the precinct is full of single-family homes owned by middle-class, two-income families, get a volunteer who knows about taxes and schools.

As we said, finding a precinct volunteer is not that hard, and many local campaigns get plenty of offers of help from local people. The real problem is making the best use of them. The volunteers want to help, but too often they are not given any direction, nor are they incorporated into the overall campaign strategy. I have seen a lot of campaigns founder even though they had a lot of people willing to work because the volunteers were not given anything to do.

One of the first tasks, which the volunteer coordinator should do early in the planning stage, is to prepare a list of general duties for the precinct volunteers. This list should be written out, or in the computer, and given to anyone who asks, or is asked, to be a precinct volunteer.

When the volunteer coordinator talks to the volunteers for the first time, he gives them the general list of duties but also tells them what the target number is for their individual precinct. Tell the volunteer you need 250 votes. Or say that you expect to lose the precinct, but if you can limit your loss to only 50 votes, it will actually be a victory. By telling them what you need, you give them a specific goal to shoot for.

Then go over with them the list of duties that describes exactly what they can do to help to meet the target. A sample list for a typical campaign might read as follows:

1. Circulate nominating petitions
2. Put up yard signs
3. Sell tickets to fund-raiser
4. Hold a coffee at their house
5. Arrange coffees in other homes
6. Go door to door passing out literature
7. Work the voting place on election day

The exact nature of this list of duties will vary depending on the overall campaign strategy and local circumstances. What is on the list is not as important as having all necessary duties and responsibilities listed so the precinct volunteer knows precisely what is expected.

Talk to the precinct volunteer and find out if there is something on the list he or she cannot do, or hates to do, like trying to raise money. There is no sense in trying to get a commitment for something they won't do anyway. But do get a commitment for the things the precinct volunteer can do, and try to get another volunteer to fill in so that everything gets done in that precinct. The volunteer coordinator keeps a list of the things that each precinct volunteer is scheduled to do and makes an occasional phone call to check on how things are going. When each task is accomplished, the coordinator checks it off.

Always listen to the volunteer about any suggestion he or she thinks might be helpful or would work because of the special circumstance of that particular precinct. If the volunteer says there is a nursing home with 200 residents, an important task would be to see that the residents are registered to vote. Then he would get applications for absentee ballots for some residents and arrange transportation to the polls for others.

Listen to the volunteer when he says that certain things will not work in his area. Going door to door is one of the most common ways to campaign, but in some neighborhoods a stranger at the door is threatening. In one precinct every year they close off the street and have a block party, which is by local custom absolutely nonpolitical. A candidate showed up, against the advice of a local volunteer, and it probably cost her 100 to 150 votes.

One of the main reasons for getting a local person to be precinct volunteer is that they know the area and the people. You can rely on that knowledge and capitalize on it. In one neighborhood, a family lost everything in a fire. A boy of about twelve had been badly burned on the arms, and the neighbors were taking up a collection for the family. The candidate, who had grown up in hard times and whose own family had once been burned out, was sympathetic and wanted to send a check. He cared, but he was afraid his donation would look like he was trying to buy votes. His precinct volunteer said to give her cash. She took the money to one of the women organizing the collection and said the donor wished to be anonymous. The volunteer knew this woman was the biggest gossip in town, and sure enough, within a week everyone had heard that the candidate had cared enough to donate a large sum but that he did it anonymously. Tell the volunteers what you need from them, but do not forget to listen to what they say they can do for you in the race.

Once you get it straight about what you expect from the volunteers, the next step is to give them the tools to carry out their responsibilities. Prepare a precinct packet for the volunteer that contains the materials needed to do each of the tasks.

Using the example from above, the list for the precinct volunteer sets out seven general tasks plus the special nursing home situation. The precinct package for this volunteer should contain the following:

1. A street map of the precinct
2. Nominating petitions with instructions for circulators
3. A list of the registered voters
4. Candidate's brochures—campaign literature
5. Instruction sheet for going door to door
6. Scheduling forms for coffees
7. Yard signs
8. Voter registration and absentee ballot applications

This is where having a good volunteer coordinator pays off. Every campaign runs into snags and snafus. The precinct packet should include yard signs, but suppose they are not printed yet. The coordinator gets the packet out but keeps a tickler to remember to get the signs out when they do come in. The coordinator makes sure the special items, like the nursing home absentee ballot applications, get to the volunteer. The coordinator checks, calls, consults, pushes, nags, and sees that which is promised to be done gets done.

The coordinator also listens to the precinct volunteers because, of all the people involved in the campaign, these volunteers are closest to the voters and have the best idea of how the campaign is going. Invite them to come to the staff meetings so the campaign manager and the candidate can learn how things are going. If things are going well, it is good for morale and gives the campaign momentum. If things are going badly, changes can be made.

You may not be able to get a worker in each precinct, or you may get someone who promises but does not deliver. This happens. But getting volunteers in as many precincts as possible, giving them a list of things to do, and having the volunteer coordinator follow up and help them get it done is probably one of the surest ways to win.

Let's go back to our sample precinct with its target of 250 votes and compare it with our sample list of precinct volunteer duties. Let's assume that each job gets done and that contact is made at 170 households according to the plan. We would estimate it as follows:

Responsibility	*Votes*
1. Circulate nominating petitions	25
2. Put up yard signs	20
3. Sell tickets to fund-raiser	5
4. Hold a coffee at their house	15
5. Arrange coffees in other homes	10
6. Go door to door passing out literature	75
7. Work the voting place on election day	20
Total	**170**

Each contact results in 1.5 votes. We assume 1.5 votes per household because, as we have said before, each contact generates not only the vote of the person contacted but also the vote of family members and friends. If this precinct volunteer does 170 contacts at 1.5 votes, one can expect 255 votes. There's your target number, and if you reach your target number in each precinct, you will win. Look at the things on that list. All of them are fairly easily accomplished by any precinct worker. This is a very workable list of duties for a precinct volunteer.

Perhaps the best way of analyzing the importance of the precinct volunteer is to look at it from your opponent's perspective. Suppose you have a volunteer in each precinct who is out in the neighborhood working for you on a person-to-person basis as planned. How is he going to beat you? Not with money, not with mailings, not with radio or television. If you are reaching the voters on a personal level, no impersonal medium can compete with that. One volunteer per precinct is the surest way to win.

Once, while speaking to a group of teachers, I was asked, "What is the most effective political tool?" The question threw me for a minute because I did not know what she meant by "tool." But after a few seconds, it occurred to me. The most effective tool in a local campaign is the manila envelope.

All of these precinct volunteer tasks when taken together are time consuming and will take a lot of work, but each separate task is manageable. If the volunteer has a manila envelope filled with a list of things to be done, instructions, and a packet of the materials needed to get them done, he or she is prepared to go out and do the job. Given a time frame of eight to ten weeks, the precinct volunteer has time to polish them off one at a time. As each item on the list gets done, and as the volunteer goes on to the next, your campaign is that much closer to winning.

Inch by inch, row by row. This is how you win.

⤑ PART III ⟻

CAMPAIGN PROCEDURES
AND TECHNIQUES

In Part I we talked about planning and doing all the things you need to do to prepare for a successful race. In Part II we discussed organizing the people in your campaign and how to make the best use of them. Part III is about the procedures and techniques for reaching the voters.

There are various methods for getting your message out to the voters, such as newspapers or direct mail, and we have a chapter on each one of these various methods. While it is helpful for you to learn about each method, the typical candidate is not likely to use all of them. As you read, try to think which of these techniques would be most suitable to your race.

There is no right way to campaign. There is no true rule for campaign conduct that applies to all campaigns except possibly the rule that says: Do what works. What works, or at least what has worked in the past, has usually been a blend of several techniques. In your race, you may want to do a little of one technique, like mailing, and a lot of another, like radio. Or perhaps, because of local conditions, you may do just the opposite.

The whole idea is to tailor the techniques to your individual campaign. Some campaign techniques, such as television, are very expensive. Other techniques, such as going door to door, take an awful lot of time but are the very cheapest ways to campaign. In deciding which one may be most effective in your race, you have to first decide whether you have more money or more time. In selecting which one is most appropriate for your race, you are limited to whatever resources are available, whether it be time, money, or volunteers. You will not be able to do everything you want to do, so you will have to emphasize the things you can do.

We have a chapter on each of the major campaign methods and each chapter contains a lot of suggestions about using that technique effectively. Some of the suggestions will obviously be unworkable, and those you can reject out of hand. Other suggestions, however, might be of some use, so think about using them. All of these techniques and procedures will work, but you will probably not be able to do all of them. What you will be able to do, though, is to use a little of this and a little of that to successfully reach out to the voters with your campaign message. As you read, try to think about how you can apply each suggestion to your race, perhaps with some minor modification for local conditions.

17

LITERATURE: THE CAMPAIGN BROCHURE

Even in literature and art, no man who bothers about originality will ever be original. Whereas if you simply try to tell the truth, you will, nine times out of ten, become original without ever having noticed it.

—C. S. Lewis

A political old-timer once told me about a brochure he did. Because his family was Italian and he grew up speaking the language, he was put in charge of doing a brochure in Italian for Franklin Roosevelt's 1944 campaign. The designer did a beautiful three-color cover, a silhouette map of Italy with a drawing of Roosevelt's profile superimposed on it. While walking through an Italian neighborhood, he saw some people standing on the corner looking at the brochure and wanted to hear their comments, so he wandered over to eavesdrop on them. What he heard shocked him.

"*Dove Sicilia?*" ("Where is Sicily?") The designer had the Italian peninsula but had left the island of Sicily off his beautiful drawing. Most Italian Americans have their roots in that island. It was a great-looking brochure, but bad politics.

The campaign brochure is the fundamental item of your campaign. That one piece of literature is what you will use to reach most of the voters. Some people will not read political literature, even when you put it in their hands, but many voters do. They do not study it carefully but will scan it to get an idea about the candidate and where he stands.

It is often said that people don't know who they are voting for, and in many cases that is true, but there are a lot of voters who want to know about the man or woman they are voting for. They will look at a brochure, see what the candidate says, and make a decision based on that. These thinking voters are only about 5 to 7 percent of the whole, but they take their citizenship responsibilities seriously. Although they may think of themselves as being Democrats or Republicans or Independents, they are not locked into any ideology. When they get into the privacy of the voting booth, they vote on what they know and like, or dislike, about the candidate. About two out of three contested races are decided by a margin of less than 5 percent, so it is these thinking voters who decide most elections. These are the people you are trying to reach with your campaign brochure.

There will probably be ten or twenty other names on the ballot, and though voters will read your brochure and think about it, they will not give it much time. So your brochure has to be short, precise, and readable. It also has to be planned, written, designed, and printed early in the campaign.

DESIGN

Here are a few suggestions about what to consider in designing your campaign brochure.

Readability.

In designing your brochure, keep in mind that it has to be readable. "Readability" is a term used in publishing to describe the combination of form and content. A piece is readable when it has content that is interesting to the reader and is designed in a style that is attractive to the eye. Using a larger print, for example, is one aspect of readability. Around forty, about the time people begin to vote regularly, even people who have had good vision become a bit myopic and have to start wearing glasses. Voters are not going to squint and try to read your brochure. It does not have to be like a large-type Reader's Digest book, but larger lettering makes it easier for people to read.

Short sentences are easier to understand than long sentences and make any written document more readable. Newspapers are readable because journalists use short, simple sentences. Write like a journalist. Lawyers write in legalese using long run-on sentences. Don't write like a lawyer! I once found a sentence in a brief that was 207 words long. I had the urge to order that the lawyer be thrown into jail for contempt and held there until he could diagram the complete sentence on a blackboard. He was not doing his client any good, and you will not be doing yourself any good unless you use short, readable sentences in your brochure.

No Artsy-Craftsy Stuff.

The first rule in both art and politics is to keep it simple. You may get a volunteer who has some design experience, and who may offer to design a brochure and come up with something full of curves and curls—the kind of thing that will win an award at an art exhibit. Avoid that, and go with a simple design and plain lettering. This is not to say designers are not helpful but only that you are not producing art. You are conveying a simple message.

Being in the business of politics, I look at political literature all the time and examine it a lot more closely than any voter. I am amazed at how often, particularly with first-time candidates, the brochure seems to be cluttered and confusing.

I am not against creativity. I have used good artwork in my literature very successfully, and I have included a sample in this chapter. True art, however, exists for itself, independent of any other purpose. Artwork in political literature is subservient to the message. If the brochure looks good and catches the eye but does not get read, it may be good art but bad politics.

Colors.

A psychologist at the University of Iowa did a study that found that colors affect moods (e.g., primary colors, such as red, induce aggression, while soft colors have a calming effect). Somehow this study ended up on the desk of Iowa's football coach, who immediately ordered that the visiting team's locker room be painted mauve. That weekend the Michigan coach arrived with his team, took one look at the locker room and had Michigan's blue and yellow banners strung up all over the place. It seems he read the study, too.

This apocryphal story does make a point: the color of your brochure can affect the reader's perception of the candidate. Pick a color scheme that is as simple as possible. Colors are expensive because each color is printed separately, so using three colors means three passes through the press. The section on computers discusses using computer graphics to design your brochure, and look at various options. Whatever color scheme you choose, however, use it consistently throughout your campaign. If your brochure is basically blue and white, your yard signs should be blue and white and so should the name tag you wear.

White is important because of the so-called "white space." The mechanics of vision are such that the eye sees the background and perceives the letters as holes in the background. A person standing alone on a white sand dune is more visible than one standing in a forest. A word or a phrase is more readable if it is surrounded by white space, so use a lot of white space in your brochure.

I would add as an afterthought that yellow and black are contrasting, eye-catching colors and these kinds of signs seem to stick out more than other political signs. However, I have barely seen a candidate who used that color scheme win. I do not know why that is, but I'm just throwing it in here as a bit of conventional wisdom.

Photos.

Your brochure might have your picture in it. It is not absolutely necessary, but people will want to see what you look like. If you do use a photo, it should be a simple portrait-type photo taken by a professional photographer, or at least a very skilled amateur. Always get some extra prints because you may want some for a newsletter, newspaper ads, and so forth. You may want to add some other photos to your brochure, such as one of you and your family and another one of you standing in front of the dump you're campaigning against. Using photos can enhance the overall look and readability of your brochure, but the decision to use them is entirely subjective. And again, you can rely on your computer guru using digital photos.

The Brochure Test.

When I first ran for office, I got several brochures from past elections and asked people which one they liked best. Almost everyone picked one or the other out of six samples. Both were quite similar. I designed my brochure using a similar layout and color scheme.

Today, you can use a computer to make up samples of your brochure. Try five or six different layouts, using different colors and fonts, and test them out. If you get a consensus of opinion on one style, use that. A good-quality computer and printer can produce a brochure that is camera-ready—that is, good enough so that the printer can use it to make the offset printing plates. Or the printer may prefer to receive your brochure on disk.

Mailability.

If you are planning to mail the brochure, it must be printed to comply with post office requirements. Before you start to design the brochure, go to the post office website, which we have on the CD-ROM. The site is called Business Mail 101 and it has all the details relating to a bulk mailing, such as the cost options, the size and type requirements, and even a section about creating a sample piece and seeing how much it will cost. It will explain about the Optical Code Reader, OCR read area, and bar code clear zone. Basically all bulk mail is sorted by scanners. A certain area in the center of the address side of the piece must not have any printing in it so that it can be scanned. This is the OCR read area. The bar code clear zone is on the lower right corner and cannot contain anything but the bar code. The size of the OCR read area and bar code clear zone depends on the size of the piece being mailed.

If you are using your own bulk mail permit, the permit number must also be printed. We will talk more about bulk mailing in another chapter, but your brochure will be printed up long before it is mailed. When you begin to design it, you have to think ahead and be sure that it will meet the postal requirements.

We began this book talking about planning, and this is a good example of what we are talking about. In June, when you are designing the brochure, you have to be thinking about the mailing you are going to do in late October. Thinking ahead, integrating each strategy and aspect of your campaign into the overall plan is how you win.

There is one important point that has to be mentioned about designing and printing the brochure. Most states have laws against anonymous political literature. The purpose of these laws, usually called disclaimer laws, is to prevent distribution of anonymous, and often scurrilous, campaign material. It gives voters a chance to look at the source of the political material and use that in evaluating it.

Warning!
You Cannot Rely Only on What We Say Here!

Almost every state requires that any candidate, party, or political group who produces any piece of literature designed to affect the outcome of an election must print the name and address of the person or group on that piece of literature. What is required, exactly, depends on what state you live in. In some states, you can get by with "Paid for by the Candidate." In others, you must have the complete name and address of the campaign committee and treasurer (e.g., "Paid for by Comm. to Re-Elect Woodrow, P.O. Box 192, Shaeffer, IN 64378, Mac Steward, Treas."). You will have to find out what the rule is in your state and follow that rule. There is no way around this requirement, and most states have heavy fines for failure to comply. Be sure to check your state's requirements.   ✦

CONTENT

The content of the brochure should, like the design, be simple and straightforward. Voters prefer to vote for a real live human being and will want to know a little something about you as a person.

Put in some personal biographic information, particularly those items that show you are concerned about the same issues as the local voters. If you are running for the school board, the fact that you have two kids in school means something. Be sure to mention biographical information that certain segments of the community can identify with. For example, if your suburb is divided along the lines of old-time residents and newcomers, you might want to mention you graduated from the local high school. Your membership in the local temple tells the voter one thing, your membership in the local gun club tells them another. The general purpose of the personal biographical data in your brochure is to let the readers know that you are one of them.

You will also need a section on your qualifications for the office. This part of the brochure is kind of like a résumé. If you are going after that job, the voters are going to want to know why you think you are qualified for it. When we talked about picking the office you want to run for, we suggested that you seriously ask yourself why you think you can do the job. Write down those answers in this part of the brochure.

Tell the voters about your formal education or your special training in the area. Tell them about your experience or former jobs that make you qualified to do this one. Mention your work in related public service areas such as being a volunteer for some agency or serving on some local committee or board. If you have held an appointed public office such as the local housing authority, put that in your brochure.

The third thing to remember in writing your brochure is the campaign theme. This theme is the basic principle, the underlying concept, or the slogan of your campaign. The theme should be prominently featured, in large letters and perhaps in a different colored ink. "My campaign is about Better Schools." Or even more simply, "Better Schools!"

Again, remember the importance of planning. Since the brochures have to be printed months before election day, it is important to plan your campaign theme. You will use that theme in your brochures, in your speeches, when you talk to people, over and over again. For the voter who merely glances at your brochure, that message should strike his eye. "Better Schools!" For the voter who has heard of you, the theme reinforces what he has heard. "Better Schools!"

Everyone is for better schools, of course, so you cannot forget the thinking voter, the one who will read your brochure to see what you have to say, how you plan to make the schools better. Your brochure should have a short statement of how you plan to handle the duties of the office.

Your theme might be better schools, but better schools means different things to different people. Better schools might mean a new junior high, or a new chemistry lab. Better schools might mean smaller class sizes and more classroom teachers, or fewer administrators and mandatory testing. Better schools might mean more taxes, or better use of revenues without any new tax increases.

Your campaign theme is only a kind of shorthand for what you as a candidate stand for. Your brochure must have a statement of not only what you are for, but how you hope to accomplish it. It need not be long, but it must contain enough specific details to reach and win over the thinking voter.

SAMPLE

In several of the chapters and appendixes I have included forms and worksheets for you to copy and use. It would be impossible, because of the variety of offices and candidates, to prepare a brochure worksheet. So instead, I am including a sample of my courthouse postcard, a very effective piece of political literature. I have used this basic piece successfully several times, and I would like to show you how it was integrated as part of the overall campaign strategy.

When I first ran for the appellate court, the main problem was that the district was quite large, almost as big as New Hampshire. It was made up of fourteen counties, each a separate community with its own newspaper, and there were thirty-two radio stations. There tends to be a voter fall-off even in local judicial elections, and it is much larger in judicial district races.

I had good name identification because the retiring judge was Gordon Gray (spelled with an *a*), but the voters did not think the district appellate court had anything to do with them. My race was not a local race although the appellate court hears appeals in each county's courthouse. I needed a local connection, and settled on the local courthouse, which in almost every small community has some institutional significance.

From an artist, I bought the rights to drawings of all the courthouses in the district for the front of my postcard. A typical card looked like this:

This does not look like a piece of political literature at first, but it does meet all the criteria I have mentioned. It is attractive, but the art does not distract. Instead, it enforces the idea of law and judges and legal things. It is nice to look at and conveys the very important message that I am a local judge, one who is associated with their local courthouse, one of them. The color scheme is simple, brown ink on buff paper, which suited the soft tones of the drawing—and it suited my budget because one-color printing is cheaper.

The back of the card looked like this:

There is no photo because I do not like them. The theme, Re-elect Judge Grey, is featured prominently. There is a short statement of qualifications, but no policy statement because judges are not permitted to make policy statements. Note also that there is a printed bulk-mailing permit number and a space for addressing.

This was a very simple piece, and people liked it. I was asked for extra copies. One of the cards was put into a time capsule for the tercentennial in 2076 so the folks then could see what the old courthouse looked like. Nobody was really interested in the political blurb on the back, but nonetheless they took those extra copies and passed them out to people who at least glanced at the back and read my name.

As simple as this card was, and as cheap as it was to print, it still had all the basics and was very successful.

In doing your brochure, make it basic. Use a simple color scheme and a readable design style. Say a little bit about yourself, your experience, and about what you as a candidate are for. Feature your campaign theme, but give the thinking voter a short statement of how you plan to accomplish your goals. Do not forget the disclaimer required by law.

In doing your brochure, make it basic but keep it simple. That's what works.

✦ 18 ✦

GETTING A
GOOD MAILING LIST

It is not enough to aim; you must hit.

—Italian proverb

I had a hard time trying to decide whether to call this chapter "Getting a Good Mailing List" or "Getting a Good Voter List." I decided to use "mailing list" because it more accurately describes the kind of list you will have to come up with. The typical list of registered voters is comprehensive and includes every registered voter in your district. If you have plenty of money, you can use a list like this and mail to every voter. This is one strategy but may not be as effective as other alternatives. Your mailing budget might be better used to target only certain registered voters but to mail to them twice. A good mailing list is smaller than a list of all voters but better because it is cheaper and more effective.

We will talk about how to get a list, but first, as always, we begin by talking about planning. To plan a mailing campaign you have to think about the "five Ws" of news reporting, but in a different order—Why, Who, Where, What, and When.

Why do you want to do a mailing? This is the primary question to be answered. Analyze your overall campaign strategy and see how a mailing coincides with your goals. If you are a first-time candidate trying to establish name identification, mailing a brochure with your candidate photo, background, education, and experience may be just the ticket. If this is the case, you may want as large a list of voters as possible. If there is a complex issue in the race and the voters need to learn the underlying facts, a mailing can get that information to them. But in this case, a smaller list of those voters who will think about complex issues may be more effective.

The size of the mailing list is determined by the purpose of the mailing. There are dozens of reasons for doing a mailing, and we suggest that you begin by thinking about what you want your mailing to accomplish. When you decide at the outset what you hope to accomplish from the mailing, it narrows the time it takes to do it and the costs involved. All direct mail is targeted, and picking a target group of voters is the first step in concentrating the mailing effort. The answer to "why" tends to suggest the answers to the other Ws, like Who or Where.

Doing a mailing to every Who every Where may not be a bad idea in a small race, if it is not too expensive. If you decide to go with that strategy, you will need as comprehensive a list as possible. If that is too expensive, you have to target the group most likely to vote for you. For example, it may be more effective to target the voters in only one township who are most upset with the incumbent. A good mailing list for this strategy is a list of only the voters in that township.

Virtually every mailing strategy is always a question of getting the right kind of mailing list. There are two ways of doing this. One is to get a prepared list and to cut it down to tailor it to your race. The other is to start from scratch and build your own mailing list to include everybody you want to mail to. We will discuss getting a prepared list first.

Generally speaking, lists of registered voters are readily available from the elections office, but that's as easy as saying restaurants serve food. Although every state has computerized voter lists, each state has different methods of making these lists available. Let me give you a couple of examples. In Kentucky you can order from the secretary of state a list of registered voters sorted in street order within precinct. These lists have the name, address, age code, party, gender, zip code, and a five-year voting history of every registered voter in the precinct. In Maryland, you can tailor your request for a list very specific to your race. Maryland has these options:

AREA
Statewide (All counties & Baltimore City)
Single County
Multiple Counties
District: Legis., Cong., etc.:

TYPE
County Voter Walking List
Registered Voter List (Basic list with no voting histories)
Voting History List by Election Type and Date (Select type[s] & year[s] below)
Election type: Gubernatorial Primary, Gubernatorial General
Presidential Primary, Presidential General
Election years: 1992, 1994, 1996, 1998, 2000, 2002, & 2004 are available

VOTER INFORMATION
All years, Specific year(s)
All Voters - Male - Female - By Age Range - By Registration
All Party Affiliations, Specific Party
Active Voters, Active & Inactive Voters

One of the requirements of the Help Americans Vote Act (HAVA) is that the states maintain a central database for all registered voters, which means that all elections offices have such data. How hard, or easy, they make it for you to access that data varies from state to state. At the Oklahoma site, I could not find anything at all, but I'm sure the data is available somehow.

As with a lot of other things I have written about in this book, the How and Where of getting a voter list depends on where you live. You have to find out what is available in your area. Buying a list from the elections office is not the only alternative. Ask your old hand where to get a list. Your local party may have a good list that is available to candidates. Some professional mailing houses have lists, but these can be expensive. As an election official in the Florida secretary of state's office said to me, "There's a whole cottage industry of lists out there." Getting a computerized voter list is not difficult. Making it into an effective mailing list is not difficult either, but it is an important step in the local race for office.

This is where your computer consultant comes in. Somebody once asked Michelangelo how he could carve such beautiful things out of stone. He said it was easy—"You just start with a block of marble and cut away everything that is not art." The job of your computer "artist" is to begin with a prepared mailing list and to cut away all those names that won't get you votes.

For those readers who do not know about databases, a short explanation may help. Each bit of information about the voter is kept in a separate category called a field. Party affiliation, for example, is one field. There is also a field for the ward—Ward A, Ward B, Ward C, and so on. The list you buy from the elections office will list all voters in all wards, Democrats, Republicans, and Independents. If you are running in a Democratic primary, you can tell the computer to produce a list of only those who are registered as Democrats in the party affiliation field and only those who are listed in Ward A in the ward field. Press a button, and the computer will print out a list of every Democrat who lives in Ward A. If you get this list printed out on adhesive address labels, you are ready to mail to every Democrat in Ward A. This is how computers are used to do targeted mailings.

A computer can sort out the special kind of voter you are after. I was told about a small county that had a tax levy on the ballot. The opponents got the general voter list from the board of elections and the list of all property owners from the tax office, both on computer disks. The tax office disk also contained information about which property owners had a senior citizen exemption or an agricultural exemption. Using some kind of computer wizardry, they merged the two lists and came up with a list of all voters who paid property taxes. From that list, they created a shorter list of all the voters who were senior citizens (people on fixed incomes) and all voters who were farmers (people who pay taxes on a lot of land). With that list they did two separate mailings to this special group, and the tax levy lost almost two to one. This is the kind of targeting that makes mailing successful.

Another form of computer artistry is an additive process, like painting. There you keep adding until you have what you want. This is the second way to get a good mailing list, especially in a small race.

You begin by having your computer consultant set up a database program on your headquarters computer, and you add names until you have an effective list for your district. Throughout the campaign, you keep adding to the list. People you have met and talked to. People who the volunteers have talked to. Friends and relatives of yours, and friends and relatives of the volunteers. Quite often this list can be expanded by looking at smaller lists of names where you might know someone—members of your church or union, for example, or people who showed up at your high school reunion. If anyone shows any interest in your campaign at all, his or her name goes on the list. If, in going door to door in a neighborhood, you get a favorable reaction at some houses, you can add more names to the list.

You may add names as issues develop in the race. In one area, a usually pro-labor Democratic incumbent took a stand against a large building project. His Republican opponent somehow got the membership lists from the local trade unions. He added the name of every bricklayer, carpenter, electrician, and plumber who lived in that area to his mailing list, and did an effective mailing (he won).

In building your list, the more names you can add, the more effective your mailing will be. The list you prepare yourself is more time consuming because you have to have volunteers who can type in all the information in all the fields. It may not be as big as a voter list that has been cut down, but it does target people with whom you have some connection or identification. That smaller list may be as effective because it is more precisely targeted. Whether you cut down a prepared list, or build up your own list, targeting is the key.

Preparing a list, or perhaps lists, from the voter information list is a major task for your computer expert, who must have the know-how and equipment to do it. All this takes time. First you have to get the voter list. Then you have to convert it to your database program. Then you have to decide on a strategy. Then the expert has to come up with a list or lists to carry out the strategy. All the computer work relating to making up a good mailing list has to be done long before the election, but your computer consultant cannot even begin until you have planned and budgeted a strategy. You have to start early to get a good mailing list.

We will talk about the What and When of mailings in the next chapter.

✧ 19 ✧

DOING A MAILING

Neither rain, nor snow, nor sleet, nor dark of night shall
stay these couriers from their appointed rounds.

—Homer

To do a good mailing there are several steps. The first
is to integrate your mailing into the overall campaign strategy, which we have already talked about.
The second step is to get a good mailing list which, we also
discussed. The third step is to talk to someone at the post
office about how to do a mailing. The people there are very
helpful, and most larger post offices have a bulk mail specialist—standard mail as the post office calls it. Get a copy
of the publication *An Introduction to Mailing for Businesses
and Organizations*. We would recommend that you get all
the information on bulk mailings at their website, which is
on our CD-ROM.

The USPS website, called Business Mail 101, is not only an
excellent source of information, it is a tutorial on bulk mail. The
site lists the links which tell you about the relevant criteria:

Learn about bulk business mail.
Learn how to qualify for bulk rates.
Find resources to help you prepare your mail.
Learn how to design a mail piece.

Find out how to get an address list.

Choose the right postage method for your mailings.

I would strongly urge any candidate to look at this website before making any decision about doing a mailing.

While this chapter discusses the how-to aspects of doing a mailing, your campaign might be able to bypass much of what is discussed here. Mailing service companies can handle most of the work involved in doing your mailing. It is often too expensive in a small race to pay to have things done, but bulk mailing companies are different. Although they too cost money, they often save you enough in postage to pay for their services.

If your mailing strategy is to mail out 7,000 pieces using the nonautomation bulk rate of $.289 per piece, the cost is $2,023. If you add in the cost of the permit, $160, and the annual fee, $160, the total cost of the mailing is $ 2,343. If you use a mailing service, you can use their mailing lists and their permit, and those 7,000 pieces can be mailed at the automated enhanced carrier route rate of $.138 per piece, or $966. The reduced postage cost allows the mailing service to do the printing and still make money. If, for example, the mailing service charges $.38 per piece for printing and mailing, their fee for 7,000 pieces would be $2,660. Thus, for a net difference of $317, you can have access to their precisely targeted mailing list and save an enormous amount of time and volunteer labor.

Mailing service companies can be found on the Internet and are listed in the Yellow Pages under that title, but be sure to shop around. In doing research for this third edition, I was amazed at the wide variety of prices quoted. One service would take my list on computer disk, mail to the Rs or to the Ds, or both. They would use their bar-coding software program to barcode it, get it CASS (Coding Accuracy Support System) certified (approved by the post office), and print all addresses for 16.6 cents per piece. Another quoted a charge of 17.5 cents per piece, but added extra charges for their computer time and CASS certification, so that the final cost was almost 18 cents per piece. The mailing service industry is very competitive, and if you shop around, you ought to be able to find one that will do exactly what you want at a reasonable price.

Here is what you want. You bring them your targeted voter list on a disk and your brochures printed so that there is a clear OCR (optical code reader) area and bar code zone. They do the rest. They print the bar-coded automated addresses, including the permit number, box them, and deliver them to the post office on the day you want. A lot of mail services are printing shops that do mail service as an adjunct to their business. You can take your sample brochure to them and get a price not only on the printing but also the mailing. If you can get this done at a reasonable price, it will be a big boost to your campaign. Check out the mail service option before deciding on any mailing strategy.

If you don't use a mailing service, there are three options—automated bulk mail, nonautomated bulk mail, and personal mail. Whichever you choose, your brochure must be suitable for mailing in that category, so before printing, be sure they are post office compatible. That means that before your brochure is designed and printed, you have to talk to someone at the post office or get the information at the USPS website, Business Mail 101.

That website is excellent, so anything I might say would be repetitive and probably not as accurate. A lot of what follows can probably be better learned at the website, but I feel I should discuss some matters.

AUTOMATED BULK MAIL

Long ago, the post office decided that if all mail were prepared within certain well-defined parameters, it could be processed automatically. The post office also decided, as a matter of policy, that it would help people and advise them on how to meet those parameters. Their website does just that.

There are a lot of regulations. On the address side of any automated piece, there must be a clear OCR read area, which is that space that contains no printing except the address. The bar code clear zone is similar; it is an area at the bottom right-hand corner. If you want to mail a simple sheet of paper folded in three, one side is open and the other is on the fold. You can't use staples to seal the tri-fold and get the automated rate; you have to use round adhesive tab stickers. If you do use tabs and the fold is on the bottom as you view the address, you can use one tab. But if the bottom is open, you have to use two tabs. While these regulations may seem petty, the fact is that staples screw up the scanners, and if the bottom side is open, the flaps often get caught in the machinery. There are good reasons for the regulations, and whether you can see those reasons or not, you have to comply to get the best rates.

The bar codes themselves come in various forms, the best one being the eleven-digit enhanced carrier route bar code. This allows the scanner to sort and bundle by carrier route. That bundle goes directly to the carrier, and the mail is already arranged in the same order in which the carrier walks the route. If you have a computer list, you can buy a bar-coding software program for about $40 and make up your own enhanced bar-coded mailing list. Once you do this, however, you must have it CASS certified. The Coding Accuracy Support System is a free service. You send in a bar-coded list, and they certify it as being accurate. The mailing services all have their lists CASS certified.

I could go further into automated mail requirements and techniques, but I cannot give you all the regulations. The thing to remember is that if you are considering using automated bulk mail, you should begin with the Bulk Mail 101 website. If you still have questions, check with the post office's bulk mail specialist. I have always found the people at the post office to be helpful, but there are a lot of regulations.

NONAUTOMATED BULK MAIL

You can still save money on your mailing by using nonauto-mated bulk mail. This mail is not read by machines, so the requirements are not so exacting, but there still are requirements. For example, nonautomated bulk mail must be presorted and bundled by zip code when you take it to the post office. Again, talk to the post office bulk mail specialist before deciding on this option so you can be sure your mail will meet the requirements for the discounted rate.

Nonautomated bulk mail is not addressed by computer, so each piece has to be addressed. One way to do this is to buy preprinted mailing labels. There are computer programs, like Avery Label Pro, which will take a database list of names and print out an address label for each name. These computer-generated labels can be purchased from private companies. Some elections offices will sell them to candidates, but there are other, less expensive sources. Some political parties have label lists that they make available to their own candidates at nominal cost. Having a computer-generated address label list simplifies the nonautomated bulk mailing process. The computer prints out sheets of stick-on address labels, and the volunteers just peel them off and stick them on the piece to be mailed.

Voter lists usually have the names in each precinct in alphabetical order. Your computer expert can rework that data so that all the names with the same five-digit or nine-digit zip code are printed on one set of labels. Having the address labels in this form eliminates the need for sorting; they are just labeled, bundled, and ready for mailing. Using computerized voting lists and label programs is just one more area where having a volunteer who is good with computers pays off.

But you might not have a computer whiz or even a computer. The only real alternative for a campaign without computer-generated address labels is to use hand addressing. Using volunteers to hand address is cheaper, but you still have to comply with the postal regulations about presorting, bundling, and so forth. And you need a system for organizing a hand-addressed bulk mailing.

The best way to do hand addressing is to use the manila envelope system. Take the entire mailing list and divide it into workable portions—about 150 to 200 addresses each. Put a copy of that portion of the mailing list into a manila envelope, along with the required number of pieces to be addressed. Also, include written instructions to the volunteer and rubber bands for bundling by zip code.

When you have broken down the entire mailing list into separate envelopes, number each envelope and prepare a master list, something like the following.

Envelope #	Volunteer's Name	Date:	Out	Due	Back
1.	_____		—	—	—
2.	_____		—	—	—
3.	_____		—	—	—
4.	_____		—	—	—

(and so on)

The volunteer coordinator uses this master list as a control. When envelope #1 is given out, the coordinator records the name of the volunteer and the date on the master list. This is repeated for each envelope as it goes out. The coordinator checks off each envelope—and, of course, thanks the volunteer—when the envelope comes back in. As the mailing date nears (be sure to allow time for sorting and bundling), the coordinator contacts those whose envelopes are not back yet and nudges them a bit. If there are still some envelopes not assigned or finished, the coordinator may try to get another volunteer to do another envelope.

This envelope system is primitive, but it can be very effective. In 1982, before computer labels were widely available, I used it to do a mailing of 84,000 postcards in my fourteen-county district. It required over 380 manila envelopes, a huge master list, over a hundred volunteers, and a really efficient coordinator, my wife.

Bulk mail is cheaper because you do a lot of the preparatory work for the post office, but to do that work, you have to be organized.

PERSONAL MAIL

Bulk mail works, but nothing is as effective as a personal letter. For the large campaign, bulk mail may be the only route, but for a small campaign without a lot of money, nothing is as effective as the personal letter. By a personal letter I mean a real letter with a stamp on it, written by a real, live person using a pen. This kind of letter gets read!

It would be great if a candidate could write a personal letter to each voter and ask for his or her vote, but realistically speaking that is not possible. Nonetheless, in a small local race personal letters are a particularly useful way of getting votes. Personal mail—first-class mail—is expensive, but when it is targeted in a local race it can be a powerful vote getter.

One personal mail technique is simply to have your friends and volunteers write letters to their friends, asking them to vote for you. You ask the volunteer to write ten or fifteen letters, then give them the literature to accompany each letter, and blank envelopes. You ask them to pay for the stamps, so the mailing is done with little cost to the campaign.

Using this system tends to lead to duplication. Since the friends of one volunteer may often be the friends of another volunteer, avoid duplication by circulating a master voter list early in the campaign. Each volunteer takes the list, looks for names of friends, and addresses an envelope to each one. These names are then checked off the list. Then the list is passed on to the next volunteer, who addresses her envelopes and checks off more names. Having the master list circulated is not only a control against duplication, it is a subtle way to get the envelopes done. Later, as election day approaches, the volunteer writes a personal letter and puts it in the addressed envelope.

Try to get the volunteers to put the stamps on the envelopes at the same time they are addressed. This applies subtle psychological pressure. I don't know why it is, but people hate to see a stamp go to waste. If the envelope is addressed and already has a stamp on it, the volunteer is far more likely to write the letter and bring it to campaign headquarters for mailing. Do not have the volunteers mail the letters themselves. Ask them to return the stamped letter to headquarters so the letters can all be mailed out together. There is no reason why they should be mailed out together—it is just another way of making sure the letters do, in fact, get written.

The personal letter can and should be short, especially if the volunteer has to do twenty of them. For example:

Dear Mary,

    I met with Joan Taylor, and I am working for her because I think she would be a really good supervisor. I'm sending you some information on her. Please look it over. We ought to have a woman like her on the board. Ask Charlie to think about voting for her, too.

                           Best,
                           Cathy

P.S. If you want to send $5 or $10 to the campaign, we could really use it. Make your check payable to _____.

Whether you are pushing for passage of a levy for a new library or trying to create name identification, this person-to-person contact—this endorsement of the issue or candidate by someone they know—is very effective because voters like to be sure they are making the right choice.

Another personal mail technique is what I call the computer-generated noncomputer letter. It is expensive but really works. It is a blend of all the things we have talked about, as well as a refinement of them all. Let me explain by giving an example.

The computerized registered voter lists you obtain from the elections office often show how people voted in past elections—whether they voted in the primary or only in the general elections, or if they voted only in the presidential race years. By looking at these records, you can see, for example, that John Smith voted in every election—every Democratic primary and every general election. His wife, Mary, however, never voted in the primaries. She is an Independent but regular voter, and it is pretty certain she will go to the polls.

The computer volunteer uses a grading system to create a priority "mailability" list for all voters. Independent voters who vote in every election may be given an "A," and these voters are put into a separate file. Regular Democratic voters are put into the "B" file, and regular Republicans into "C," and so forth, according to however you have prioritized the voter you want to reach. This does take a lot of time, but it actually is a savings because you are going to mail only to those Independents who are likely to vote. Every voter marked "C" or lower is money not spent—but also, perhaps, not wasted.

With this ultra-refined "A" list, you do an "A" letter—one whose content is directed to the Independent voter. Compose it on nice stationery. Use a letter-quality printer. Type the body of the letter, and then save it. Merge the "A" list addresses into your word processor. You can then call up the inside address from the list, do the greeting, and have the computer type in the body. Most word processors have a "Type Envelope" command where the inside address is typed on an envelope. The envelope and the letter are then put together for signing. The candidate signs each letter, using blue ink, so it contrasts with the black ink of the letter and looks like a real signature. This personal letter is then put into the envelope and stamped. Use the biggest and brightest commemorative stamps you can find to create an attractive letter.

I want to add a warning here. If this letter even vaguely appears to be anything but a personal letter, it will be perceived as junk mail and may be discarded without being read. If done right, however, these letters can work wonderfully. People are pleased and often amazed to get a personal letter asking for their vote. As a result, the candidate is no longer a name but someone who has personally asked them for support.

It takes an awful lot of work just to do a hundred letters this way, but think back to what I said earlier in the book about the narrow margin of victory. One or two hundred votes may be that margin. If you have targeted the two hundred "A" people who are most likely to vote, when they go to the polls they will see two names. One of those names will mean something to them because it is the name of the candidate who wrote and asked for a vote, so they are very likely to give you that vote.

If you have enough money, you then do a "B" letter—one whose content is directed to the faithful Democrats. These personal letters can be very effective.

TIMING

The timing of the mailing is a matter of strategy. If you are trying for name identification, an early mailing might be best. If it is an issue-oriented mailing, a later mailing—after there has been discussion in the newspapers—might be more appropriate. There is always a question of when to mail, and as a corollary to that, how many times. If the campaign can afford more than one mailing and can get enough volunteers to do it, two mailings, like two heads, are better than one. The first should be done fairly early, such as twenty to twenty-five days before the election, with the follow-up coming as close to the election as possible. If you are only doing one mailing, timing the mailing date is important.

Don't forget that it takes time for the mail to get delivered. According to the post office, 99.2 percent of first-class mail gets delivered the next day, but let me make a point here about the timing of bulk mail. In theory, bulk mail gets a low priority from the post office. In practice, automated bulk mail, which is barcoded with the eleven-digit bar code, will be processed and sent directly to the carrier arranged in the same order of the route delivery. This automation speeds up bulk mailing so it is processed very quickly. Nonautomated bulk mail takes longer.

The post office is pretty good about getting political mail out on time because it has no value after election day, but there is also a lot of it around election time. If your mailing is all going to the same zip code, it can take a relatively short time to be delivered. If it is all going to one three-digit prefix, such as 606__, it can take a little longer. If you have several zip codes—such as 60601, 60701, and 60801—it will take even longer. When you initially talk to the post office about designing your brochure, rates, and so forth, ask how long it will take for your proposed mailing. Ask for a suggested date—a deadline, so to speak—for mailing. Be sure to put that date (or dates, if you are doing two mailings) on your campaign calendar. Work back from that date to set other deadlines for each task in the mailing process that has to be done.

Let me repeat one thing about mailings. Mailing requires organization, and organization requires planning. If you are going to do a mailing, all the decisions about Who, Where, and When have to be made months ahead of the election. In almost every chapter in this book, I have said, "Plan ahead." To do an effective mailing, I say, "Plan way ahead!"

✢ 20 ✦

RADIO AND TELEVISION

Something terrible happens to music once you turn thirty-five.

—Dave Barry, *Miami Herald*

TARGETING

As Dave Barry's laconic comment above points out, about the time you turn thirty-five, popular radio stations are no longer playing the kinds of music you grew up with. Radio, like the other mass media, is directed primarily at the eighteen to thirty-five age group; stations play the garish cacophony that the younger generation likes, which means you have to hunt for a station that plays your kind of music. From the media's standpoint, however, you are not seeking them; they are seeking you. In a word, this is called targeting.

Targeting means directing your advertising only at those people whom you want to reach. If you sell a product such as aspirin or mayonnaise, which almost everyone uses, advertising directed at the largest number of people is likely to be most effective. If you sell hot tubs or service transmissions, you need to reach a smaller, but still definite segment of the buying public. If you sell fine wine or cigars, the number of buyers becomes even smaller. Remember how we pointed out in Chapter 2 that the target number of voters in a city of 35,000 was only 3,300. That is only 9.5 percent of the population. Since a lot of people don't vote, targeting is the most critical factor in radio or television political advertising.

There are three kinds of electronic media: radio, cable television, and broadcast television. Let's begin with broadcast television. Advertising on broadcast television is just too expensive for a local race. Broadcast television is a mass medium, perhaps the "massest" of the mass media. It reaches the largest segments of the population, but it is not very good for targeting voters unless your target is several hundred thousand people in a metropolitan area.

If you can afford $1,500 or $2,500 for one thirty-second television commercial, that is the political big time, and you would do well to employ a professional political and media consultant. (By the way, if you have a great pile of money you want to blow on an election, the author of this book is available as a consultant at $2,000 per day, plus expenses!) If you cannot spend that kind of money, you have to forego broadcast television advertising.

You can also forget about any broadcast coverage of your campaign as a news event. Television news is often trivial. Many television stations are concerned primarily with ratings; news divisions are operated as entertainment enterprises, and serious news is often not entertaining. I once tuned into a Charleston, West Virginia, station to get the results in the mayor's race, and the lead story that night was about a house fire. One long-time politician told me that television news coverage for local elections is subject to the live boy/dead girl rule. He said, "Television news will not mention a local candidate unless he is found in a motel room with a live boy or a dead girl." A bit cynical, and perhaps out of date with the many women candidates, but his statement is not too far from the truth.

With broadcast television out, the other two mediums are cable television and radio. Radio can be very effective in a local political contest. Dave Barry's problem of having to hunt for his kind of radio station happens to everyone. It is an important consideration in using radio in a political campaign. The big radio stations are part of the mass media that seek to appeal to the younger population in general, but the population in general does not vote, particularly the younger part of the population. Small radio stations are directed toward smaller, specialized segments of the population, and often these smaller, more specialized groups are the very ones you want to reach.

I have used radio in every campaign and recommend that you think about using it in your race. Cable television is becoming more adept at targeting, and we will talk more about that later in the chapter, but let's concentrate on radio for now.

Radio is effective because of its selectivity. I read a study about the Blue Nun radio marketing strategy in a radio industry publication. Blue Nun is a brand of German white wine; the desire was to get a larger share of the American market. Using only radio advertising, and using only those stations that dry white wine drinkers were likely to listen to, Blue Nun was able to create name brand identification in almost 80 percent of the wine-drinking population. You can obtain that same kind of effectiveness and selectivity in your radio advertising.

The first thing to do is to find out what kind of radio stations are available in your area. If you live in a small town, of course, there will be only one or two stations, but in a larger, more metropolitan area, there may be many different stations. Some metropolitan stations, however, operate like small-town stations by catering to listeners in one or two suburbs, or on one side of town.

Many libraries have a publication called *Television and Radio Yearbook*, which lists every station in the country and includes a brief description of the station, its range, and its format. The station's format may be hard rock, soft rock, easy listening, MOR (middle-of-the-road), country, talk, sports talk, and so on.

As an alternative, you can check the Yellow Pages and ask each station listed to send you the station's demographics, rating information, and a rate card. The demographic information tells you what sort of programming format the station follows, the range of the signal, the kind of people who listen, where they live, and so on. The rating information tells the number of listeners in the area and the station's share of the market.

But you have to take the station's data with a grain of salt. In one city with four radio stations, three claimed to have a 40 percent share of the listeners aged eighteen to thirty-five. Nonetheless, the station demographic data does tell you a lot about the people who listen to the station and is fairly reliable because it is based on the results of rating service company data.

You are not interested in stations that play what you like to hear; you want stations that your target group of voters listens to. Stations differ not only by format but also in their appeal to listeners in subcategories. There are ethnic stations, Spanish-speaking stations, Christian stations; even these specialized stations are further subdivided (e.g., Spanish-speaking Christian stations). There might be two radio stations whose listeners are primarily black, but one may go after the young blacks with rap, while the other plays blues and jazz—classic black music, if you will. Or a station might have a strong news and information format in morning drive time and talk shows for the rest of the day. As a rule of thumb, no matter what kind of voters you are after, there is probably a radio station that targets that group.

A second rule of thumb in radio is that the cost is relatively cheap in comparison to other media. Radio is cheap because federal regulations require all licensed stations to give political candidates favored treatment. The regulations are wordy and complex, but what they come down to is this: A radio station must give political candidates the same rate that it gives to its best customers. When a big advertiser buys a lot of radio time, they often are given a substantial discount. The station must sell radio time to political candidates at that same discounted rate, and this is often a bargain for the candidate.

When you get the station demographic information, the station should also send you a rate card. The cost of any radio ad depends on when it is broadcast because that determines how many people are listening. The rate card tells the price for various times. The 7:00 to 9:00 a.m. morning drive time period is expensive because many people listen to radio while driving to work. Evening drive time, about 3:30 to 5:30 p.m., is a little cheaper, and late-night hours are very cheap because usually only third-shift workers and insomniacs are tuned in.

The prices on the rate card quote so much for a sixty-second spot in morning drive time, a bit less for evening drive time, and so on. There are also prices listed for each time slot for thirty-second spots and ten-second spots. Look for the lowest price listed in any given time slot; this is usually the political rate. As a general rule, most stations will sell radio advertising to political candidates at the lowest price quoted on the rate card for that length of spot in any given time slot. This is the deepest discount they give.

Because regulations are subject to change, what I say here may be a bit out of date. There is talk in Congress of requiring radio station licensees to provide some free time to all candidates, but I doubt if it will ever pass. You will have to check with your local radio station about the exact rates.

After you have the demographics and the rate card, the next step is to work a radio campaign into the budget. Although radio is cheap, you need a lot of it. They say a person has to hear a radio ad twenty-five times before the message sinks in. We recommend that you do at least thirty spots, in the same time slot, spread out over several weeks. For example, three weeks before the election, you have one spot per day in morning drive time. Two weeks before, you have two spots a day in the same time slot. The last week, you go with three a day.

With the cost of a radio ad program in mind, you then have to sit down and make some budget decisions to see if you can afford this kind of program. You should try to buy your radio time early. Although the stations have to give you their best rate, they are only allowed so many minutes of commercials per hour. Once the commercial time allowed for that hour is sold, it is no longer available, even to political candidates. You probably want to buy the morning drive time slots just before or after the local news, but so do all the other candidates. Radio stations have to avoid any kind of favoritism and sell political advertising on a first-come, first-served basis.

Having found a particular station through which you can reach a certain group, and having decided how much it will cost, you now have to decide what kind of radio spots you will use to go after those votes. So let's talk a little about the content of the radio spots and how to produce them.

Radio spots are usually either ten, thirty, or sixty seconds, and we recommend that you use only thirty-second spots. Radio as a medium is best used to deliver a short, precise statement. Sixty-second spots are too long and tend to bore people. A radio spot is not a public debate, but rather a chance to make a short, informative point about yourself. Ten-second spots are too short.

To illustrate, read aloud the previous paragraph. It should take you about twenty-five seconds. Then add the disclaimer, "Paid for by the Committee to Elect Grey"—that's your thirty seconds. A thirty-second radio spot gives you some name identification, a chance to emphasize your campaign theme, and the opportunity to say a few words to the voters. A thirty-second spot allows about eighty to ninety words, which is really not a lot.

It is critical, therefore, that your radio ad copy makes your point as simply and precisely as possible. If your point is name identification, you will want to repeat the name several times. If your point is the candidate's stand on a local issue, you only have eighty words to describe the issue and take a stand on it. This is hard to do and precisely why writing radio copy is a professional specialty.

In writing the copy for your ad, sit down and write at least three versions of what you want to say. If you can have several people each write a separate version, so much the better. Read them aloud, and listen to how they sound. See if one doesn't have a catchy phrase. See how long it takes to read each one. Then edit, cut, and paste phrases together until you have a short, clear, punchy thirty-second spot. You may plan a big radio campaign with seventy-five or one hundred radio spots, and this means you will have to produce several different spots and rotate them. If you do, use the same method for writing each one.

Once the copy is written, you will have to have the ad produced on tape. Many stations, particularly the smaller ones, will produce the ad for you in their studio. You give them the copy, and one of their announcers reads it. Some stations construe the FCC regulations so that the candidate himself must speak in order to get the preferred rate. In that case, you must go to the studio and read the ad.

Some stations require that you produce the ad on a master tape and give it to them. In such a case, you can have the ad produced in a professional studio, and this can be expensive. If the radio station requires you to produce the ad yourself, that should appear on the rate card. Find out about this because this must be taken into account in setting up the budget for a radio campaign. Check the Yellow Pages for a recording studio; ask for their prices, or ask the station advertising salesperson to recommend a good, cheap recording studio.

Some amateur musicians have recording facilities and equipment that may not be state of the art but can still be used to produce a fairly high-quality tape. You might be able to find such a semiprofessional set-up like this, and get the musicians to help you record your ad. Ask around.

If you are producing the tape yourself, try to get a reader with a good radio voice to read your ad. People sound different on tape, so have try-outs among the volunteers to find a person with a nice voice. Check with the local university's drama department or a nearby school of communications for someone with a good radio voice. Your tape can be produced by nonprofessionals, but it cannot sound nonprofessional. I have heard some radio ads produced by amateurs that were quite good.

One final point about radio. We have suggested you plan early, write early, produce early, and buy time early so that you have the times and the tapes done and ready to go as the campaign heats up. One further advantage of radio is that it can be used for a quick response. If you have your times paid for and your ads ready, and a week before the election some new issue or event comes up, radio can be used very effectively to combat your opponent's tactics. You can produce a new radio spot and have it on the air almost overnight. If a new issue seems to be developing, or if you get a sense of the public mood on a question of policy, you can capitalize on that by taping a new radio ad tailored to the new development. Ulysses S. Grant was most famous for always carefully preparing for each battle, but he himself said that the way to win is to "maneuver according to circumstances." With a well-prepared radio campaign, with the spots paid for and the ads already taped, you will be ready to maneuver as election day approaches.

CABLE TELEVISION

While radio is a very cost-effective means of political advertising, cable television as it is developing may be more effective. Radio, even a small station targeting a select group, is still a broadcast medium. Cable companies are wired to their subscribers within a defined geographical territory. Cable television goes only to those people wired to the system, and so you know exactly where they are and where your cable ad is going.

Most local cable companies do local commercials. The cable company picks up the signals from satellite television networks, which include national, mass-market commercials, but they reserve a few minutes of advertising time during each hour for themselves. The local cable station produces and sells local commercials for these minutes. Compared to broadcast television these cable commercials are very inexpensive, but price is not the only advantage. Cable television is good at targeting voters and is getting better at it.

Geographically, if there is just one large cable company that serves almost the entire metropolitan area, you run into the same two problems with large broadcast stations—it is too expensive, and it does not target. The trend is toward one large company per metropolitan area, and as the one cable company grows larger, it loses its ability to target a specific geographical area. The ability to target a specific area is a significant factor for many advertisers, not only political candidates, so as the trend toward the larger cable company continues, many of them are starting to use what they call split-zone transmission. They split their local cable signal so that one commercial will appear on the television sets in one zone while, at the same time, a different commercial will appear in another zone. They use electronics to do the same kind of targeting that is obtained when there are several local cable companies. Not all the large metropolitan cable companies are doing this now, but it is a coming thing. Even if a cable company becomes dominant in the metropolitan area, there are a lot of advertising dollars to be won or lost depending on its ability to be able to target areas within the greater metropolitan area.

Demographically, cable is good at targeting by sorting out people by program content. We have about one hundred and sixty channels on the cable in our house, but my wife and I don't watch half of them. Our kids don't watch half either, but it is an entirely different half. That is the beauty of cable. Since the content of many of the channels is directed toward very specialized audiences, you can make some valid assumptions about the viewers. Who do you suppose watches the Home and Garden Channel? Probably older people who own their homes, who want them to look nice, and are willing to spend time on them. Who are most likely to be registered voters who vote in local elections? Older people, people who pay real estate taxes and want to live in a nice area and so are concerned about their community.

This is a very unscientific demographic analysis, but it shows how the demographics of a cable channel may come close to matching the demographics of your target group of voters. News agencies are almost always good spots for local candidates. In some areas, the auto racing channel might be better than the golf channel. I was amazed to find that nostalgic television channels featuring reruns of past shows like "Gunsmoke" and "The Rockford Files" reach a lot of people age thirty-five and up in many areas of the country.

For the actual demographics on any particular channel in your area, go to your local cable company and talk to them. The Cabletelevison Advertising Bureau has several publications available on its website: http://www.onetvworld.org/main/cab/research/productusage/index.shtml

I am including a few of their suggestions about what you should discuss with the local cable company.

1. The area you want to reach.
2. The demographic characteristics of the residents, such as age, income, occupation, etc.
3. Coordination with your other advertising efforts so they complement each other (e.g., your campaign theme ought to be prominently featured in both your brochure and your cable ads).
4. Your budget and their rates, including the cost of producing one or more commercials.
5. Timing and scheduling, which is very important in political ad buying because, like everyone else, you want them scheduled around election time.

There is, as in radio, a preferred rate for political candidates required by federal regulations for cable television. Generally speaking, almost everything I have said about radio applies to cable television except that the need to buy early is probably more crucial with cable.

The price of any cable television ad, like radio, is based in part on the time of day it is aired. You can buy prime time, the evening hours when people watch television, but it is the most expensive. The cheapest is called "BTA"—best time available—which really means any time available; they just stick them in whenever there is some time.

Unlike radio, the price of a cable ad is also based in part on the program in which it appears. This, in turn, is based on the number of people likely to be watching that program. You may not need the most expensive channels, because you may want to target a relatively small group. Because of Senator Dole's age, for example, President Bill Clinton used spots on MTV, the rock music channel, to successfully woo the younger voters. You might be better served by going with CNN, the Weather Channel, the Speed Channel, or the Home and Garden Channel. The thing to do is to sit down and think first about who you want to reach and then, after looking at the cable company's demographic data, think about which channels are most likely to reach them.

I recommend using thirty-second spots on cable. Although I think a well-done sixty-second spot on television does not bore people, a lot of other knowledgeable people do not agree. A sixty-second television spot, however, does require what the people in the trade call high production values. That means it has to look and sound good. You probably cannot produce a television spot yourself. You will either have to go to a production company or pay the cable company to have this done, and this does tend to increase the cost of cable advertising.

Prepare the copy for your television ad the same way we suggested for radio ads—that is, try several versions, read them out loud, cut and paste, and so forth. Television is a visual medium, and the people producing the spot will tell you how to dress and give you other valuable information. These people are experts in the business, and you would do well to rely on their advice.

In a very unscientific survey done by the author, it appears that the cost of a thirty-second television spot is about 1.5 to 3 times as much as a thirty-second radio spot. Cable prices vary tremendously, so be sure to check them in your area.

Do not just buy radio or cable time. Try to figure out which medium and which times will best fit into the overall strategy. Compare the relative cost of each one. You may want to do only radio or only cable, but you might work up a joint radio-television advertising program. A really good advertising program might involve using several radio spots in morning drive time and one or two cable television spots with the evening news.

As always, your campaign and your plans will be limited by what you can spend. So start with the rate card and the demographics and see where you want to target and who you want to reach. Give radio a budget priority. Give television a budget priority. Plan ahead. Buy ahead to get the time slots you want.

Radio or television is like everything else in your race— how well you use it depends on how well you plan for it.

21

NEWSPAPERS

If I had to live in a society without laws or a society without newspapers, I would choose the society without laws.

—Thomas Jefferson

N
o matter where you live in the United States, there is probably one large newspaper that dominates in the market area and sometimes even throughout the whole state. There might be another smaller competitor, but very few cities have two major daily newspapers. Starting about thirty-five years ago, newspapers began to consolidate. The major newspaper in a city bought out the competition, or they merged, or entered into a joint production agreement where they shared printing and distribution facilities. Whatever the method, the smaller newspaper withered away after the consolidation. Sometimes the smaller newspaper simply went broke and stopped publishing.

Whatever the cause of this phenomenon, the fact is that most cities now have only one major newspaper, which is a mass medium. Their circulations are usually in excess of 100,000 and their advertising rates are too expensive for the typical local candidate. Not only are the rates expensive, since the newspapers themselves are aimed at the mass audience, they are not very useful for targeting particular voters or areas.

As the big fish were eating up the little fish and getting even bigger, however, a hole developed in the newspaper business. Since the bigger papers had to concentrate on larger, metropolitan news, local news tended to be neglected. The events, disputes, ordinances, and goings-on in any one neighborhood or suburb were not important enough to the readership in general to be covered, even though they were quite important to the people in the local area. This lack of local coverage opened a new area for the small local newspaper. Consolidation put a lot of reporters and editors out of work, and these people knew how to write and print a newspaper. As a result, as the major newspaper grew to a dominant position, many of the old-time local newspapers expanded and some new newspapers sprang up to fill in the gap in local coverage.

The Chicago area is an example. The *Chicago Tribune* is the dominant paper and there still is the tabloid *Sun Times*, but both these newspapers have very large circulations that justify the expensive rates. If you are running in suburban DuPage County in the village of Naperville, however, you need to reach the people there, and money spent to reach voters elsewhere in metropolitan Chicago is useless.

In Naperville, there is the *Naperville Reporter*, which publishes stuff like the local police blotter and the high school news releases. It is important for the residents to know which of their neighbors got busted for speeding or DUI or whose kids made the honor roll. This paper also covers local news such as zoning changes, school board meetings, or sewer and drainage problems—the events that may well be political issues.

Much as Naperville is only one of dozens of suburbs around Chicago, the *Naperville Reporter* is only one of dozens of local papers in that area. There are over sixteen hundred dailies and thousands of weeklies in the United States, and there is probably one in your area. In some areas, there may even be two of these small publications, and if there are, find out about each one.

You should be aware that these papers do get read. They are read especially by the people you most want to reach—the people who are interested in what goes on locally. Most elections are decided by less than 5 percent, so the margin of victory often lies in reaching that small percentage of voters who consider the issues and who have learned something about the candidate. Local newspapers give you a chance to speak to these voters with a substantive message.

ADVERTISING

The local paper in your area may be only a local advertising vehicle for stores in the area, one that has no reporters and only throws in copy as filler. It might be nothing more than the weekly shopping news, which is distributed free from racks on the street, but if the local merchants use it to reach people, so can you.

Do not forget the ethnic newspapers, which are usually weeklies. These ethnic papers are particularly good at reaching blacks, Spanish, Polish, Irish, and so on. If an ethnic group makes up a significant portion of the population in your district, and if the ethnic voter sees your news release or ad in his paper, he will think of you as a candidate who recognizes that his ethnic group is an important part of the community.

Since local newspapers have limited geographical distribution areas, and since the cost of newspaper advertising is based on circulation, they are doubly efficient. They target the area and the people you want to target, and do it at the least possible cost. You cannot begin to set budget priorities until you know the cost of newspaper advertising, so early in the planning stages you should go to the newspaper and talk with the advertising manager. Find out their rates. Newspaper advertising is usually sold on the basis of column inches for each day the ad runs. The standard newspaper format is six columns per page, so a one-inch ad across one column is a column inch. A full-page ad would be six columns, each about 21 inches, or 126 column inches. The actual price per column inch depends on circulation.

Ask the advertising manager if there are any discounts for larger purchases. Most papers have a flat rate per column inch, but there are substantial discounts for bulk purchasers. Some small newspapers will permit candidates to join together to buy a bulk contract at the lower rate and divide the space among themselves.

Ask the advertising manager about composition and layout of the ad. They are usually quite helpful. While the message and the copy for the ad has to be written by you, the composing room people are experienced in what looks good. They can tell you about how to use white space and photos most effectively.

The advertising department will probably remind you that under local law you have to have the political disclaimer printed on your newspaper ad, but if they do not, remember it is your responsibility to see that it is printed with your newspaper ads. Check your local elections law on this.

Be sure to ask about the deadline for advertising copy, which is usually longer than the news deadline. Advertising copy is often set up two or three days ahead of time, and space is left for the news to be inserted on the day of publication into what is called the news hole.

While you are at the paper talking to the advertising manager, also talk to the editorial manager who, at a lot of small papers, is often the same person. Find out about the paper's editorial policies and how they treat the coverage of the local election contests. Some papers are more interested in local politics than others. Ask about how they handle news releases and when the news deadline is. Find out if they run letters to the editor, and what their policy is on running them. Not many of these smaller papers endorse candidates in local races, but find out if they do and on what basis they judge the candidates.

If they have a reporter or stringer who covers local elections, introduce yourself, give him your campaign headquarters phone number, and tell him to call any time there is a question. If something comes up during the campaign close to the deadline, you want to be sure the reporter is able to contact you for your comments before the story is printed.

The whole idea is to get the people at the paper to know you because they will be hearing from you regularly. You will be sending out news releases as an important part of your campaign. Before we talk about news releases, though, I want to make a short digression here to talk about something that will make the editors hate me.

If you plan to use newspaper advertising, don't wait until the election day approaches to buy space. Try to make a contract with the paper for as many inches as you can afford, and pay in advance. Do this well in advance of election day—at least several months. During the campaign you will be sending out news releases, but if the paper never runs them, call up the advertising manager and complain. Threaten to cancel the ads and ask for your money back. He will hate to lose the sale, and will suggest to the editor that your releases be given some play. Never lose sight of the fact that a newspaper ad might cost $100, but news releases carry your message to just as many voters and are published for free. The editors will hate me for telling you this, but for a small newspaper on a tight budget, this is an effective technique for your campaign.

THE NEWS RELEASE

To redeem myself with the editors, I will tell you how to do a good news release, because a good news release makes the editor's job much easier. Lost revenue or not, if your news release is no good, it will not get published.

Put yourself in the editor's shoes. He has on his desk not only your news release but at least a dozen others all seeking to have that news release published. He has to come up with something that is interesting and readable in a limited amount of time under the deadline, and he has only as much space as is allowed for the news hole that day.

Looking at the news release from the editor's point of view tells you exactly what a good news release should be. It should be in the proper form—short, readable, and legitimate. We will discuss each of these separately.

The proper form for a news release includes the name of your campaign, a contact number, the date, and a release date, something like the example below.

GREY FOR JUDGE

July 22, 2007   Contact: 555-3247

For Release   (daytime number)

    ____ immediately

    ____ (date)

Copy: The body of the news release follows.

Each of these details serves a definite purpose. The editor wants to know the source of the news release, and the date. If you want to ask the paper to hold off using the release, you can request a release date, but the editor does not have to honor it. The contact number is important. If they have a question about the release, they will not run it until that question is answered. If they can make a quick call to the contact number and resolve the question, they might run it. If they have no one to contact, into the wastebasket it goes.

We suggest that you have the news release form preprinted with all this information either in the computer on a macro or on a disk. If you don't have a computer, prepare the basic form and run off copies. When a news release is being prepared, you already have the form with all the details—just type in the date and copy for that release. A news release can be e-mailed or faxed, but it is good to check to see if the paper has a preference.

A news release is short. By short we mean absolutely no more than one page, and if it can be managed, only one or two paragraphs. Two-page news releases do not often get printed, and three-page news releases may not even get read. The editor only has so much space, and if he can fit your short release in, he might. If he has to edit it, he will worry about getting complaints that he has changed the meaning of the release. If he has to see about cutting it down to fit, he probably won't bother. After all, he probably has another news release, a short one, on his desk ready to use.

A good news release is readable in both form and content. Use double space in typing and leave wide margins. These margin spaces are needed to write in editorial corrections, to add diacritical marks, and to give directions to the composing room. Do not type on both sides of the paper because all editing is done on one side only. Not only is using both sides of the page confusing (and by definition too long), many papers use scanners to get the copy into their computers for composing. Typing on both sides of the page screws up the scanner. For those of you concerned about waste and the environment, remember that sending out a news release that will not get printed is waste in its purest form. Stick to one page and to one side.

In writing the copy, try to use the old Who, What, Why, Where, and When mandate of old-fashioned journalism. Put all the information in the first paragraph, and expand in the following paragraphs. Edit and proofread your news release carefully. Always have at least two or three people review the release for errors or ways to make it more readable. The whole idea is to have it in such a form that the editor can read it, accept it for publication, and send it on to the composing room with as little effort from him as possible.

If you are sending a release to an ethnic foreign language newspaper, send the release in English, but if you can include a translation it helps. Not only do you control the translation, you have a much better chance of getting it published. When

I ran for the supreme court, I had a volunteer who translated my releases for several Spanish papers and another volunteer who did the same for a weekly Hungarian paper. I speak enough Spanish to know that the releases got good coverage. The Hungarian paper even endorsed me, I think. I speak no Hungarian, but they used my photo and featured my name in an editorial, which I assume said nice things about me.

Finally, a good news release is legitimate. If a news release contains news, if it is fair comment on an issue before the public, if it is something of interest to the readers or community in general, a news release is legitimate. If it is just an attempt to get some free publicity or to get your name in the paper, it is not. If your mother announces that you are a nice person and that she will cast her one vote for you, this is not a legitimate news release. If you speak at the Women's Business and Professional Association luncheon and take a strong stand in favor of the local school levy, that is a legitimate subject for a news release.

A good news release is in proper form—short, readable, and legitimate—but during the campaign it is often difficult to come with new releases. One good way to have legitimate news releases is to write them up ahead of time, weeks before the campaign gets hectic. In August, you have plenty of time before the November election, so sit down and write some news releases then. This is not as hard as you might think. In planning your campaign, you know that certain issues are going to come up and that you are going to raise other issues. In August, you know that somewhere down the line you will be taking a strong stand in favor of the school levy (or perhaps against it). So prepare a news release on that subject, and then in October, when you get invited to speak somewhere, you publicly state your position. Then you go to the prepared news release, edit it briefly to fill in the relevant details, and send the release out.

One advantage of prewriting your news releases is that it focuses your campaigning—that is, it makes sure that you do take a stand on the issues you want to raise. If you have a prepared news release on the topic, you will remember to raise that issue. One further advantage is that the closer it gets to election day, the less time you will have, so having a news release prepared helps. It is hard to sit down in the middle of a campaign and knock out two or three paragraphs for a news release. If you have prewritten releases almost ready to send out, the job is more easily done, and the release itself is better because you wrote it when you were not under a lot of pressure. Some things will come up that you are not prepared for, and trying to do releases on those will be difficult enough.

You may want to send a photo along with the release if you have one. I had a student photographer trailing around after me during one campaign, and she took photos of a lot of my campaign appearances. We included her photos with several of the releases and a lot of them were printed. You should, early in the campaign, send a short biography and file photo to each newspaper so they can have it on file. When you do send any photo to a newspaper, always write the names of the people shown, the kind of event, the date, and the name of the photographer on the back.

The important thing to remember is to send out news releases regularly. It costs about 60 cents, including postage. If you send out ten releases and only two get printed, that is an awful lot of publicity for six dollars.

We began by talking about how the big newspapers drifted away from neighborhood and local coverage, and how the void was filled by smaller papers. There is a trend in some areas by some big papers to get back to covering local news. As local advertisers began using the local papers because they targeted a smaller area, the major papers reacted by creating special local supplements for the suburbs, inner-city areas, or other identifiable neighborhood markets. They set up local offices in the area or desks in the main office and assigned reporters to those areas. Find out who the reporter for your area is and try to meet with him or her to introduce yourself. Give the reporter a short bio, a photo, and all the numbers where you can be reached. Get the reporter's phone and fax number and find out exactly to whom news releases should be sent. It is usually that reporter.

LETTERS TO THE EDITOR

A final point to be discussed is the Letters to the Editor feature. This is one of the most widely read parts of any newspaper, and not only that, these readers are the persons most likely to vote. If your local paper has a Letters feature, be sure to take advantage of it.

Virtually everything we said about news releases applies to letters to the editor. They should be short, be typewritten, include a phone number, and, above all, be legitimate. A letter that is nothing more than a bit of campaign puffery will not get published. One that discusses an issue, and mentions your position on it, will. Find out what your local paper looks for in selecting which letters to print. Ask the editor.

Letters to the editor can be particularly useful in focusing the campaign on issues you want to raise. In 1992, a long shot was running against a well-entrenched incumbent congressman who had bounced several hundred checks at the House bank. This was a big story in March, but the question was how to get it before the public in October.

The newcomer decided to have people, friends of the campaign, write letters defending the practice. The writers said they thought it was okay for the congressman to bounce checks. One even wrote that bouncing checks was okay because they were underpaid and it is hard for a congressman to get along on his $130,000-a-year salary. Each letter defending the congressman not only kept the issue alive, it also generated letters from outraged people not involved in the campaign. The long shot won, and although these letters to the editors were not the only reason, they helped keep this issue before the public.

To get a letter published you have to make it balanced. Do not laud your candidate as the greatest thing since sliced bread. Discuss an issue and why you are for it, then say you will vote for the candidate because he is for it, too. Don't be afraid to mention your opponent's name, but do not denigrate or abuse him. Saying the opponent is a jerk will not work. Damn him with faint praise. Say he is doing the best he can but just does not understand the problem with his limited background and experience. Or say that the opponent used to do a good job, but he has been in office too long, and we need new blood.

A political polemic will not get printed, but a balanced, well-reasoned, short letter to the editor will, and it can be a very effective campaign tactic.

A good newspaper campaign strategy will be a blend of targeted advertising; good, short news releases; and well-written letters to the editor.

In closing this chapter we would have you keep in mind, when dealing with reporters and editors during the campaign, that the election is only the beginning. When you win, they will be covering you as an elected official, so it is good to get off on the right foot. Promise them that during the campaign, and while in office, you will be accessible and honest with them. Ask them to be just as fair and as open with you.

22

YARD SIGNS
AND BILLBOARDS

What's in a name? that which we call a rose
By any other name would smell as sweet.
—*Romeo and Juliet*, Act II, Scene 2

What's in a name? In politics, having a good political name gives any candidate a tremendous advantage because voters tend to vote for names they recognize or identify with. Running against a person with a good name puts you at a disadvantage, and you have to deal with it in your planning. This is called "the name game," and we will talk first about what we mean by a good political name, and then how to deal with it.

A good political name can be defined as a name that has a positive connotation in your local area. It is a name that, all things being equal, people are more likely to vote for than not.

A good political name arises out of the typical voter's psychology. There is the thinking voter, the one who studies the candidates and the issues, but there are a lot of voters who do not. They are overwhelmed or confused by too many names on the ballot. Quite often this type of voter will see two names and not know either one. The tendency is to not vote at all, which accounts for the voter falloff in low-profile elections.

Another reaction is to just guess and pick one of the names. For the guessing voter who looks at two unknown names, if one has a positive connotation and the other has a negative or merely neutral connotation, the tendency is to vote for the name with the positive association. A positive connotation may arise out of party affiliation, or because of the candidate's sex, or whatever. It may arise because one name sounds like another (e.g., when Judge Gordon Gr*ay* retired, I won election to his seat even though I spell my name Gr*ey*, with an *e*). The candidate's name almost always has some connotation, intended or not. I remember a woman telling me she voted for Costello because she liked Italians, although it is also a common Irish name.

The name game can affect the outcome in any race, and the planning of any race must take into account which of the candidates has a good political name. Just having such a name increases one's chances of winning. Running against a candidate with a good name increases one's chances of losing.

Let me give you some examples of how important a name can be. In one Midwestern state in the 1970s, there were twelve statewide offices, six held by Democrats and six held by Republicans, but the Browns outnumbered them both. There were three Democratic officeholders named Brown and four Republican Browns. A lot of voters thought there was this one guy named Brown down in the state capitol who seemed to be doing a good job, so they kept electing him.

In one county, John Corrigan is a popular name based to a large extent on the reputation of John V. Corrigan, a well-respected, longtime politician who had a distinguished career in public service. He was so well thought of that a lot of other Corrigans, especially people named John Corrigan, started running for office. Many of the voters thought they were voting for good old John, or maybe his son, or maybe just because they knew the Corrigans were good people. Whatever the reason, the name John Corrigan had a tremendously favorable connotation among the voters. As a result, so many John Corrigans got elected that now when the people in that area discuss local politics, they speak only of "John V.," "John T.," or "John E.," because there are so many John Corrigans that they can only be identified while the surname Corrigan is left unsaid.

Perhaps the most candid assessment of the name game comes from Patrick A. Sweeney, a state representative from Cleveland who served in the Ohio legislature for over twenty-five years. The name Sweeney is so popular in Cleveland that at any given time in the last two decades there have been at least six Sweeneys holding some office locally. A reporter asked Pat Sweeney, who is well known for his quick wit, what the *A.* in his name stood for. He replied, "Another."

We may have used too many examples here in talking about the importance of a good political name, but it is a critical consideration for every candidate. You cannot change your name, of course, but the reality is that if your name is Sweeney, you have a good shot in Cuyahoga County. If you are running against a Sweeney, you have to work hard to show the voters that your opponent is "just another Sweeney."

We will discuss first the strategy to be used by a candidate who has a good political name, and then discuss campaigns where the candidate's name is not a household word.

If you have a good name, plan on using it as part of your campaign strategy. If you have a locally popular political name, you should emphasize that in your race. Having a good name will not, by itself, win the election. It is kind of like being tall for a basketball player. Being tall gives a basketball player an edge, but he still has to out-hustle the other players on the court. If you have a good name, you have an advantage, but you will still have to campaign vigorously. You will have to reach out to the thinking voter, the one who will look to your qualifications regardless of your name. With the thinking voter your name might also have a positive connotation, but you will have to reinforce that connotation with something more substantial. Nonetheless, if you do have a good name you ought to capitalize on it and include signs as part of your overall campaign strategy.

This is where yard signs and billboards come in. Signs are used for name identification and reinforcement not only in politics but in most advertising campaigns. Look at the billboards around you. Have you ever seen a billboard used to introduce a new product? Probably not. Signs and billboards are used to reinforce the consumer's already conceived idea about the product. Ford uses television to describe how its pickup trucks have strong bodies and solid suspension systems, but its billboards will only show a picture of a pickup truck and the word "Tough." The intent of the billboard is to reinforce some positive aspect. If you have a good political name, there already exists, to some extent, a favorable impression in the minds of many voters. You use signs and billboards to reinforce that positive impression.

When we talk about a good name, we mean a good name in your area. How do you know if you have a good political name? Ask around; ask your old hand. In one district, Wyznefsky might be a good name, but in another it is Wong, and in another, Williams.

Most candidates have just ordinary names, politically speaking, and your name is likely to be neutral without any connotation, good or bad. Whether you are a Wyznefsky, a Wong, or a Williams, your name is what it is, you are stuck with it. If you do not have a good political name, this has to be taken into account in planning your campaign strategy.

What you have to do, quite literally, is to make a name for yourself. The important thing to remember is that regardless of whether your name is popular or unknown, signs and billboards still serve the same function and still are only useful for one purpose—reinforcement. For the candidate who is an unknown, the first task is to create name identification and then give that name a positive connotation.

To make your name a good political name, you have to go out and meet and talk to people, and listen to them. You have to use all the other techniques such as mailings, speaking engagements, and news releases to create a positive association with your name. Then you can use signs to reinforce the positive image you have created.

You also have to assess the political value of your opponent's name. That name may already be widely identified in the district. This is a critical factor, because for the unknown who is running without a lot of money, it might be wise to not use signs at all. A better strategy might be to concentrate all your time and money on a one-on-one, person-to-person type campaign. In working out the budget, the signs might be included but would be given lowest priority. If you use signs at all, be sure you use them for a specific, well-defined purpose.

If you decide to go with signs, be sure they are integrated into the overall campaign plan. Just putting up signs may get you a few votes, but putting them up as part of your reinforcement strategy is far more effective. I have seen signs appear for candidates that I have never heard of, and I watch politics pretty carefully. The average voter is much less interested, so I presume that candidate has not done much to get his or her message out. Unless the sign stands for somebody, some principle, or some idea, it is useless. It does not mean anything.

I have also seen signs used effectively in a well-organized campaign. The candidate or the precinct volunteer went through an area talking to people and convincing some of them to put a sign in their yard. You could follow the campaign and see how well it was going by watching these signs sprout. Each sign indicated the candidate had convinced the people in that household that he was the right one for the job. Every new sign that went up reinforced the people in their original judgment of the candidate.

This is not to say that signs cannot be put up at the earliest opportunity, only that you must plan to make them part of your reinforcement strategy. During the campaign, you will be talking to the voters at meetings and coffees, doing mailings, sending out news releases, or going door to door. Until you have made these kinds of contacts, your signs will not mean much. After you have made an impression on the people you have talked to, they will now know your name and associate it with a policy or position they are for. The signs will reinforce your name and the positive connotation your campaigning has created.

Let's turn now to the minutiae of signs and billboards, the details that are always so important. We will begin with billboards because, for the purposes of this book, they can readily be disposed of. Commercial billboards are expensive. They are expensive to print and expensive to rent. They are so expensive that they are beyond the resources of the typical campaign, and we can only offer one suggestion about billboards.

If you are planning to use them, keep in mind that although they are expensive, the cost of any billboard is based on its location and the number of drivers likely to see it. I know that many do not agree with me about commercial billboards because the best billboards are very popular and have to be reserved well in advance. Other advertisers and other politicians may want the billboards you seek, so if you plan on using them, be sure you reserve them early and remember you usually have to pay for them well in advance. Other than that and except for the size, billboards are much like yard signs, and the things we say about the yard signs are generally applicable to billboards, too.

The most important quality of a yard sign is that it be readable. Let me tell you about one candidate who had the absolute worst yard sign I have ever seen. My wife and I were driving through a neighborhood of older houses, house hunting. In several yards I saw these striking signs, magenta with dark gray letters. I couldn't make out the name because the colors blended into a quivery, unreadable blob, and the signs were all set back from the curb. I saw these signs in several yards because the magenta made them clash with their surroundings, but I kept squinting and guessing and trying to make out letters. I simply could not read the name from a distance of twenty feet. I wanted to stop the car and walk up on somebody's front lawn to read the sign, but my wife would not hear of it, so I cannot tell you the name on those signs, but I can tell you they were a total loss as a campaign technique.

You might think it odd that I am telling you that you have to put up signs that can be read, but you would be amazed at the signs I have seen that are only marginally readable. The signs have to be visible and readable from a distance. In a society of human beings who tend to go myopic after age forty, visible and readable means large letters on a contrasting background that can be read from several hundred feet away.

The message on the sign itself can be brief and to the point but should contain your name in large letters and the office you seek in smaller letters. Remember also that a sign is regarded as political literature, and your state's disclaimer law may require the name and address of the candidate or his committee to be printed on the sign. This disclaimer can be in very small type.

On your signs, you want big visible type, and it ought to be done in the same color scheme as your brochure for maximum reinforcement effect. One good way to pick a color scheme and type size is to make a sample sign using colored, felt-tipped markers. Experiment with different-size letters and colors, then test the sign. See how visible it is from a distance. Take the test sign and place it in a typical location somewhere and have another person, some myopic friend, drive by and get his impression of it. Try this with several styles of sign and find out which one is most striking, easiest to read, and how big the letters will have to be. Try this with a couple of people and you will usually find there is a consensus of which sample sign is best. With that in mind, you can come up with a good design for a readable and effective yard sign.

Warning!
You Cannot Rely Only on What We Say Here!

In designing your sign, keep in mind that many communities have restrictions on the size and location of signs. Whatever your design is, it will have to be in compliance with the local law. There are restrictions on how soon before an election signs can be put up and prohibitions against them in certain locations. In some communities, signs must be on the house, while in others signs are prohibited on the house and must be in the yard. Putting signs on utility poles is generally forbidden because they cause problems for linemen, but that rule is often violated. Whatever the rules are, you must check your local ordinances for these requirements. ↞

When you have the design and colors picked out, get price quotations from local print shops. Printing, especially small job printing, is a very competitive business, so we suggest you shop around for the best price.

Have your signs printed on a good, thick, quality cardboard stock. Use an ink that is not likely to fade. Even though the life of a political sign is relatively short, the effects of sun, wind, and rain can take a rapid toll. You can get signs printed on plastic, which is more resistant to weather, but these are more expensive.

Cardboard or plastic, you want the sign to be readable right up until election day, so if you use cardboard, you may want to take steps to protect the signs. A coat of clear varnish can extend the life of a sign, and one good tip is to take the stack of signs as they come from the printer and use a roller with varnish to seal all the edges. As the sign is attached to the supports, the front and the back are also coated to keep moisture out.

The signs as they come from the printer are just flat cardboard or plastic, so if they are to be used as yard signs they have to be attached to supports. Most lumber stores sell lath (thin, flat strips of wood), which can be used for this purpose. The best way to make up the signs is to use a staple gun to attach the two uprights to two cross pieces so you have a rigid structure. Then the sign is stapled to that structure.

There are two methods to sign making. The first uses only one printed sign stapled to the frame, and the sign is put parallel to the street. This is cheaper, but it is usually more effective to have signs on both sides of the frame so that the sign can be placed perpendicular to the flow of traffic and be readable by those coming or going. In either event, the actual location of the sign when it is put up should be somewhere that is readily observable.

Political supply houses carry sign systems consisting of a horseshoe-shaped wire frame and a double-sided plastic sign open on one end. The wire frame is pushed into the ground and the sign is slipped over it and stapled. This type of sign may be a bit more expensive, but it is easy to set up, weatherproof, and usually worth the extra cost.

One final point about signs. In previous chapters, we talked about making the most effective use of your volunteers by giving them specialized tasks. Sign making is just the kind of specialized task for one or two volunteers. A lot of campaigning is paper-shuffling office work, and a person who works with his hands might feel ill at ease doing that. If you have a volunteer who is handy and has tools and a garage, you can turn the whole operation over to him. He can produce the frames, staple the signs, and seal them. He can store the signs, and get them out to people as the need arises. He can erect the signs for those who might not be able to do it themselves, erect them in a good location, and see they are firmly rooted against the wind.

Bumper stickers are really nothing more than moving signs, so pretty much everything said about signs applies to bumper stickers. I am not a big fan of bumper stickers, but some experienced politicians swear by them. When you see some idiot driver pull some incredible stunt, you have to wonder if the bumper sticker on his car is getting the candidate any votes.

Still, if you want to try bumper stickers, keep this in mind. I went to work for the Justice Department right out of law school. The head of our division was William Ruckelshaus, who had been defeated in a race for the Senate the year before. He told me that Ruckelshaus was an impossibly long name for a bumper sticker, and a short name like Grey was an advantage. Bumper stickers might be okay for Wong, but maybe not for Wyznefsky.

Before we close this chapter, we want to mention planning and organization one more time. A good name is an advantage, and signs can be used to reinforce name identification. Even an unknown candidate can use signs to create name identification and reinforce the effects of other campaign techniques. But with either strategy, there must be advanced planning.

We also talked about organizing your volunteers and said that a campaign works best if each function is parceled out to a volunteer and he or she knows what is expected. The signs are just one example of this. If you have a person who makes up all the signs, gets them out, and gets them up, you are a step closer to winning.

Signs are useful, but planning your campaign and organizing your people are still most important.

23

GOING DOOR TO DOOR

Never doubt that a small group of thoughtful, committed citizens can change the world; indeed, it's the only thing that ever has.

—Margaret Mead

All of the techniques discussed in earlier chapters cost money. This chapter is for the candidate who has very little money. While having money does give a candidate a tremendous advantage, going door to door to speak with the voters is still one of the most effective campaign techniques. If the door-to-door campaigning is done well, it levels the playing field between the rich candidate and the poor one.

Let me give you an example. A young lawyer, a Democrat, moved to a small Midwestern town to open a practice, and not long after, the local Democrats asked him to run for county attorney. His opponent was raised in the county and was well known, and it was a very Republican area. The last time a Democrat had been elected county attorney was in 1942, and according to local legend, the Republicans were so miffed by his victory that they arranged to have him drafted in 1943.

The lawyer agreed to run, but he had no money and could not raise any because nobody expected him to win. So all summer long and into the fall, he went from neighborhood to neighborhood going door to door. He did a few houses every day and talked to people, introduced himself, and left his campaign brochure. I would like to be able to tell you he won, but the fact is he did not. He lost by about one hundred votes.

It is his losing, however, that makes the point about going door to door. Everyone thought he would lose and nobody paid much attention to his quiet, steady campaigning, but as he went from door to door he was actually picking up a lot of votes. Only one person, the wife of his opponent, realized how well he was doing. She kept her ear to the ground and had a good sense of public sentiment, and around the first week in October, she realized it was going to be very close, maybe even an upset. She realized that all their signs, ads, and mailings were being overcome by this personal, one-on-one, door-to-door campaign.

So what did she do? She and her husband started going door to door themselves. In the three weeks left to them, they went to about two hundred households with registered voters, but only won by one hundred votes. Without those two hundred visits, they would have lost. Everything in politics is a two-edged sword, which cuts both ways, and we relate this story to demonstrate that door-to-door campaigning is an especially sharp sword.

Going door to door is still the most effective technique in a local election. Earlier in this book we talked about voter fatigue and voter falloff in low-profile elections and said we would talk about a way to overcome that. Door-to-door campaigning is the way.

Voters hesitate to vote when they have to choose between two names and do not recognize either one. Many simply do not vote in that race. Some will vote for a name they recognize, which is why a good political name is so helpful, but more often than not, voters will not vote for someone they don't know. If the voter has seen and talked to the candidate, even though he may not agree with everything the candidate has said, he is more likely to vote for the person he has met than for the other faceless name on the ballot.

Time is not money, in spite of what you may have heard. Money in a political campaign can expand by good fund-raising efforts. Time cannot be expanded, and the typical candidate in a local race has not only the day-to-day demands on his time like work and family but also the time demands of running for office. The real drawback with door-to-door campaigning is that it is so time consuming.

It takes time to go to the neighborhood and the street. You knock on the door, wait for a response. You introduce yourself and give the resident a piece of literature. This takes time. If he asks you a question or makes some comment, you have to take the time to talk about his concerns. Then it takes time to walk to the next house and start all over again. If you do not have money to spend, then you have to spend the time to do this.

While you can spend time, you cannot waste it. Going door to door is so time consuming that you have to plan it so as to make the best use of the time available. The Jehovah's Witnesses are the subject of many stand-up comic routines because they go door to door soliciting everybody. People who are not interested in religion, or in their religion, do not want to talk to them. Politics is the same way. It is useless to go to houses where you are not likely to get some votes.

In preparing to go door to door, you have to get a good walking list—that is, one that not only shows where the registered voters are but also indicates which of those registered voters you want to talk to. When you go door to door, you follow the walking list and go to each house on it and bypass all the rest.

A walking list can be prepared by computer, using the list of registered voters. (See Chapter 9.) The computer sorts out all the names that you want to go to. A walking list can also be done by hand using a paper printout of the registered voters on any particular street. This takes more time, but it is basically the same task, picking those houses where you are likely to do yourself the most good.

For example, if your voter list shows party affiliation, you would strike off the members of the other party and just go to the Independents and the people in your party. Or you might figure you can count on the party people, and just go door to door to the Independents. If the voter list shows how often the voter has gone to the polls in the past, you might ignore party considerations entirely, and go to all the Rs, Ds, and Is who vote regularly. A good walking list is good to the extent that it has all the right houses marked and all the wrong ones stricken off.

Not everyone you meet and talk to will vote for you, of course, but if you make a good impression on the voter and listen to what he or she has to say, they are likely to give you a vote. This is what campaigning is all about; getting people to know you. If after meeting you in person and talking to you, the voter is turned off and does not want to vote for you, let's face it, you are not likely to win and this book is not going to do you much good.

Even with a good walking list that has cut out a lot of unlikely houses to visit, you will still run into people who are not interested. Some are downright rude, but that's the way people are. In such a situation, be polite, but do not waste any more time and get on to the next house. Most people are polite, however, and even if not interested will be courteous enough to listen for a moment. Do not impose on their courtesy; make your point and be off.

The basic procedure for going door to door is this. When the door is answered, tell them your name and the office you're running for, and offer them a copy of your brochure. From then on, you have to play it by ear and be sensitive to the person. If the person seems harried or vexed and it looks like you have interrupted something, cut it short. Ask them to read the brochure, thank them, and get off the porch. If they seem vaguely interested, try to make a short plug for yourself such as saying something about your campaign theme. If they have a complaint, listen to the complaint.

If they want to talk, talk to them. When you do talk to people, try not to spend too much time at any one house. You can waste a lot of time talking to people who are likely to vote for you anyway, and even more talking about matters or events over which you as the candidate have little control. So even if you get a positive response, if it seems to be taking too much time, politely mention the other houses you have to hit and move on.

Occasionally, about as often as you run into a rude person, you run into a person who really seems interested in your campaign. They may have already heard of you and be in favor of the position you have taken on some issue. If that happens, try to involve them a bit more in your campaign. Tell them that if they are in favor of the issue, they can help out by putting up a yard sign. Or suggest that they may want to come to the next coffee in the area, and put a check by their names to be sure they are invited. You can tell them about the need for volunteers, and you may even want to give them an envelope addressed to the campaign so they can make a contribution.

In going door to door, you will find that each household is different, and you will have to wing it and adjust your approach to each situation as it develops. The whole idea is to leave them with the impression that you are a concerned, thoughtful person, the kind of person they would like to vote for.

Since it is so time consuming, there simply may not be enough time for the candidate to go door to door in the entire district. While it is not as effective as the candidate, having a volunteer go door to door is sometimes almost as good. This is where having a volunteer in each precinct is particularly useful.

One good way to do this is to have the volunteer go down one side of the street and the candidate down the other. When the volunteer finds a really interested household, she calls the candidate to come over and talk to them. I was doing this once, and the volunteer called out to me, "Larry, come over and talk to this damn woman. She won't take my advice about anything." I did not think this was the way to get votes, but the woman who wanted to meet me laughed at the whole business. My volunteer was a crusty old fishwife, but all her neighbors liked her anyway. Most of the people she talked to were willing to vote for me on her recommendation, and she resented the fact that the other woman would not take her endorsement as a good enough reason to vote for me.

A precinct volunteer knows the neighborhood, and when one of them goes out on your behalf, it is a kind of endorsement, not unlike Michael Jordan endorsing basketball shoes. The voter will associate your name on the ballot with a face, sort of like a first cousin to a real identification. You reach the falloff voter by proxy, and the precinct volunteer is that proxy.

When you think about the size of your district and the time it will take to go door to door in each precinct, it is a daunting task. If a candidate and the precinct volunteer work a street together, it is almost as effective but takes only half as much time. If the candidate cannot go door to door with the precinct volunteer, the volunteer ought to do it anyway. In our chapter on precinct volunteers, we suggested that in the instruction sheet the precinct volunteer be given a quota for going door to door. We repeat that suggestion here. Rather than having the volunteer try to hit every house, you set a definite target number. If they meet the quota, they can always do more, but it is helpful, psychologically, if they have an attainable goal to shoot for.

You may have a very large district or not enough precinct volunteers. In that case, you may want to use your other volunteers. For example, if you have a dozen college kids, you can do a sweep of a neighborhood on a Saturday afternoon. When you use this kind of system, you still have to have targeted walking lists, but you also have to maintain some kind of control not only over the areas covered but of the people themselves.

Be sure the volunteers look presentable. Emphasize the importance of being polite, courteous, and avoiding confrontation at any cost. When you give them the walking lists, also give them a set of instructions on what to do. The volunteers follow the same routine the candidate uses in going door to door. They say hello, mention the candidate's name, give them a brochure, and then try to gauge the listener's reaction. If the person appears to be uninterested or indicates they do not want to be bothered, the volunteer cuts it short, says thank you, and leaves right away. If the person seems vaguely interested, a brief statement about the candidate may be in order, and then he or she leaves.

If the volunteers get a positive reaction at any house, be sure they mark that on the list. If you are making up your own mailing list, these names should be added to that list. The candidate can use the names marked on the list to make a follow-up phone call, or answer a question, or in some way indicate his interest in the voter's concern. The candidate's follow-up contact is very effective because you know for sure the voter is interested, and it is one of the most efficient ways to use his valuable time.

When you use a group to do a door-to-door sweep in an area, it is best to have one person, perhaps the volunteer coordinator, keeping track of everybody. The coordinator assigns the streets and checks them off as they are done. The coordinator chauffeurs people about from the end of one walking list to the start of a new one. The coordinator takes care of the important stuff, such as the checkmarks on the lists for follow up, and also the trivial but necessary stuff, such as seeing that they do not run out of campaign material and finding restrooms.

Although it doesn't include the candidate, nor even someone from the neighborhood, this kind of door-to-door campaigning still gives your name something of a human face. It gives your name some identification. This is even more distant from a real identification, a first cousin once removed if you will, but still it is better than a meaningless name on the ballot.

One final point about door to door. If the residents are not at home, try to leave some of your literature, and instruct your volunteers to do the same. You cannot leave campaign material in the mailbox; it is against the law. The post office adopted a rule against doing this, because they lose money when people distribute their own stuff instead of mailing it. This was challenged in court and went all the way up to the U.S. Supreme Court. One would think the Supreme Court would have better sense, but it upheld the post office in spite of what the First Amendment says.

Be that as it may, since you cannot use the mailbox, you have to have some way of leaving your literature at the house when the people are not home. One way is to put it in a plastic door bag hanger. These are simple plastic bags with a hole cut out for hanging on the doorknob. You can buy these from a political supply house (described in the next chapter). You can also have doorknob hangers printed with your message. The cheapest and best way, I think, is to simply supply the volunteers with rubber bands and have them put it around the doorknob.

This is the final chapter of the section on campaign techniques, and throughout this section I have said that all of the various methods—newspapers, radio, mail, and so on—are good and useful strategies, and they are. I want to conclude by saying that, in my experience, going door to door is the best. It is the most effective and the cheapest. I realize that every candidate will be under terrific time constraints, but there is hardly a better way to spend your time, in a local race, than going door to door and meeting the people whose vote you want.

Go back right now and look at the section on the target number, that magic number you need to win. If you have done everything we said, and it still looks like the race is going to be close, then get out there and go door to door and get those few extra votes.

✣ 24 ✣

MISCELLANEOUS THINGS THAT OUGHT TO BE MENTIONED

Democracy with its semi-civilization sincerely cherishes junk.

—Paul Klee

This last chapter will deal with several subjects that ought to be included in any book about local politics, including a few words about things that were not discussed.

WHAT HAS BEEN LEFT OUT

This book gives the reader a comprehensive and well-organized plan for winning a local election. There are some political techniques and procedures that have not been mentioned because we do not think they work. Not everyone will agree with us about what works, and a difference of opinion is what, as they say, makes horseracing and politics, but we can give you examples of some of the common techniques we omitted and why we omitted them.

Some people think using phone banks to call registered voters and solicit their votes is a good idea. We don't. While the phone banks might make it easier for the volunteers and may have had some success in the past, telemarketers have killed off the usefulness of this technique. Millions of people have listed their phone numbers on the national Do-Not-Call list.

Because of First Amendment considerations, political phone solicitations are not banned, but if people don't want unsolicited calls, you are not likely to get votes by calling.

A telephone solicitation by friends or acquaintances, of course, is different. In the chapter on mailing we talked about having each volunteer write to ten or twelve friends. These contacts could be done by phone, although we believe personal letters are much more effective; however, this friend-to-friend type of phone solicitation might work. Phone solicitation by strangers, however, is no longer effective and might even be counterproductive and end up costing you votes.

Some people like literature drops, where volunteers go from house to house dropping off a piece of the candidate's literature. They do not talk to people. Hand delivering each piece may save 13 to 22 cents in postage, so if you have a lot of volunteers who can pass out fifty pieces per hour, you save $6.50 to $11.00 per volunteer hour. We think if you have a lot of volunteers, and they have a good targeted walking list, they can talk to twelve to fifteen people per hour. The postage savings may be less, but you are more likely to get votes this way.

What we have included in this book works. This is not to say that what we have omitted does not work, only that we have not tried them, or that we have tried them and found they did not work as well as expected. What is included is a comprehensive plan for what it takes to win a local election. Whether there might be something else you can do to win is an academic question. Doing each and every thing we suggested is sufficient to win any local election.

GIMMICKS AND GIVEAWAYS

One question we often get from newcomers to politics is, "Where do you find the companies that sell campaign gimmicks and things to pass out, like bumper stickers and buttons?" Do not worry about that; they will find you. These political supply houses have local sales representatives who check the elections office for the names of anyone who files for elective office. These sales reps will contact every candidate either by phone or by mail, flogging their wares. If they don't contact you, you can find all sorts of suppliers on the Internet.

These companies have standard products that are imprinted with the candidate's name, and the list of products is quite long. What you can get just about runs the gamut of the alphabet, and this is only a partial list.

Almanacs	Emery boards
Adhesive lapel stickers	Eyeglass cleaners
Balloons	Fans
Bookmarks	Golf tees
Bumper stickers	Hand cards
Buttons	Jar lid removers
Combs	Indexes
Calendars	Key chains
Doorknob hangers	

These items are sold by the hundreds or, more commonly, by the thousands, and there is a discount for larger orders. Prices vary, but based on some 2007 price lists, below are some sample prices:

	100	*1,000*
Bumper stickers	$125	$380
Emery boards	N/A	150
Pencils	26	150
Litter bags	N/A	152
Signs	890	2,440
Lapel stickers	N/A	214

There are even places where you can buy a complete campaign package. At one online outfit, for $599, you get: 250 bumper stickers, 100 yard signs, 100 sign frames or wires, 500 literature bags, 1,000 lapel stickers , and a 2' x 4' banner.

For $899, you get: 500 bumper stickers, 250 yard signs, 250 sign frames or wires, 1,000 literature bags, 1,000 lapel stickers, 24 campaign T-shirts, and a 2' x 6' banner.

These giveaway items can be expensive, and you have to make serious budget decisions about how much to spend on them. What you choose for your race is your decision, but we are partial to certain items. Emery boards are one of the cheapest gimmicks, and people always seem to pick them up from the tables at political gatherings. Women use them on their nails, and many men like to have one in the tool box. Litter bags are good. They are not only inexpensive, they double as doorknob hangers. Jar openers—textured rubber pieces that give you a good grip on jar lids—are popular but expensive. Pencils are good. Matchbooks are good in some areas and anathema in others. Using matchbooks nowadays may be making a political statement, but smokers do make up more than a third of the population in some areas—and smokers do vote. If Congress imposes a two- or three-dollar tax per pack, they will vote in droves. Go with what works.

We mention these items only briefly because they are not critical to a campaign, but they can be quite useful in getting the candidate's name before the people. As with everything else, you have to balance the cost against the anticipated benefits. Do not buy this stuff just for the sake of having it. Decide which of these items can best be integrated into the campaign strategy, and use that one.

WHAT IF IT GETS SLEAZY?

In the first edition of this book I proposed a law of politics in the same vein of Parkinson's Law or Murphy's Law. My law read, "The sleaziness in any political campaign is inversely proportional to the size of the election district." I then went on to talk about how presidential and congressional candidates were at least civil to each other. Things have changed, and not for the better. Politics on the national level has replaced debate and discussion of issues with accusations and acrimony. When it gets down to local politics it, too, is often "down and dirty." Too often in a small political district, the race for office dissolves into a name-calling match or an exchange of scurrilous accusations. This may well happen in your race, and we give you this piece of advice.

Avoid sleaze! Do not get involved with any kind of sleazy tactics. We say this for two very good reasons. One is that it cheapens the whole process, but the other is that it does not work. Personally attacking your opponent or his morals, habits, family, or beliefs will not get you many votes, and it is far more likely to turn off the voters to your race entirely.

We are not so naive as to suggest that occasionally something will happen during a campaign that makes your opponent look bad in the eyes of the voters. If your opponent has personal problems, it may work to your advantage.

In one race, a man was running for city council. Two weeks before the election, his wife sued him for divorce. She must have really hated his guts because she filed the divorce petition so close to the election, and it contained allegations of drunkenness, adultery, and wife beating.

A television reporter sought out the opponent and asked him to comment on how this might affect the election. Instead of attempting to capitalize on the affair, he said, "That's none of my business, and probably none of yours. The real issue in this race is . . ." I cannot remember what the issue was, but it was a great answer. He came across not only as a decent man, but he emphasized his campaign theme one more time.

I met this guy a few years later at a political gathering and learned he was not only a decent guy, but a skilled politician. He gave me a wonderful bit of advice: "You can count on the gossips." He said that most people don't care about sleazy stuff and that to bring it up turns people off. There are voters who are swayed by such things, but you do not have to talk about it. A candidate can take the moral high ground but suffers absolutely no ill effects, because the gossips carry the message to those voters who think this sort of stuff is important. On the other hand, if you try to attack your opponent, you stand to lose the voters who are turned off by sleaze. So avoid sleaze!

Your opponent, however, may try to make it sleazy. What do you do in that case? Again, it is the same mandate: *Avoid sleaze!* It may be very hard for you to do, and you may be outraged by some of the tactics pulled on you, but you do not try to fight fire with fire—or more exactly, fight mud with mud.

If attacking your opponent with the same kind of sleazy charges would work, we might recommend it. In fact, it will not. In the first place, the validity of the charges will be judged in terms of your response, and the greater your reaction the more credible they seem. Your outraged reaction will just engender more of the same kind of charges, and in the mind of the average voter the whole campaign dissolves in a childish "Did not!" "Did too!" shouting match. Using a calm denial or a wistful comment about the real issues in the election is a far better way of handling it.

It is very easy for us to pontificate about taking the high moral ground and using resoluteness of purpose when you have to deal with some very hurtful things said about you or even your family. We do not advocate that you be a patsy. Instead, we suggest that when your opponent pulls some sleazy trick that you get your revenge on the swine. The best revenge, of course, is to deprive him of what he wants most. Get him in the worst possible way—beat him in the election! But to beat him, you have to be in control.

We have spent a good part of this book talking about planning, organizing, and making things run according to a well-thought-out plan. To win you have to be in control of all the events in a campaign. If you overreact to some sleazy charge, all that planning goes right out the window. You become a trained bear. Your opponent pulls the chain, and you dance. Your opponent pulls the chain again, and you do a somersault. You cannot win if your opponent is in control.

In 2004 Kerry and the Democrats overreacted to the sleazy "Swift Boat Veterans" attacks, and the campaign at times seemed to be about the Vietnam War. In 2006, the Democrats stuck to their anti–Iraq War theme and won both houses.

If you stick to your carefully prepared campaign plan, you are in control. You have thought about the target number it will take to win, and how to reach those voters. You have planned a combination of strategies such as personal meetings, mailings, door-to-door campaigning, and put it all together in an organized manner. Why should anything your opponent says affect that plan?

If you let him distract you from your plan for winning, you may well lose. If you stick to the plan, you will probably win. It is as simple as that. No matter what kind of sleazy tricks an opponent pulls, keep in mind that as long as you maintain your sense of purpose and direction, keep emphasizing your campaign theme, keep getting your message to your targeted voters, and keep the campaign going the way you planned it, you will win.

THE SERIOUS CANDIDATE

If the reader is this far along in the book, we must presume that you are a serious candidate, so we will conclude with a discussion of the seriousness of political office. We are living in a time when our governments—local, state, and national—are reviled. Government is disparaged, while free markets are touted as the be-all and end-all. This fascination with free markets will last until the next big recession, but there is no doubt that markets work and that they are quite democratic. Markets cater to the will of the majority and, in utilitarian fashion, create the greatest good for the greatest number. Although markets are efficient, they are also exclusive and undemocratic. Being centered on the top of the bell curve, they ignore the bottom on either end. If you wear an odd-size bra or a size 14 shoe, the market is not much concerned about you.

Governments, on the other hand, must be inclusive. Being dedicated to equality and the dignity of each individual, governments must act so as to include everyone, even those at the very ends of the bell curve. Because governments are inclusive, they are less efficient than markets, especially democratic governments.

Still, there are things that only governments can do. Imagine a rocky coastline where a lighthouse would be an aid to all shipping. In a free market, no single ship owner will build the lighthouse because he would undertake all the costs, while the light would shine not only for him but all other ship owners. A consortium of owners might build the lighthouse, but they would be at a competitive disadvantage with the owners who did not contribute. To build a lighthouse, you need government action where all are taxed to pay for it and all benefit from it.

The idea that all should benefit from government action has been lost to some extent. Our governments have been so concerned about the rights of the various smaller groups at either end of the bell curve that they have lost sight of the need to adopt policies that benefit all. Schools, for example, under federal mandates have adopted policies to give special treatment to children with special problems. This is in itself not a bad idea, but concern for the special education student has so devoured scarce education dollars that the opportunities for the ordinary student have dwindled. We all benefit when we live in a society that takes care of those who need special treatment, but if that society seems only concerned with the rights of a few, the many will become disaffected. In a democratic society, when a government institution abandons the concerns of the majority, the majority will abandon that institution. The schools, the Congress, the universities, and the local governments are all falling victim to this abandonment.

If you are to serve in a government office, you must be dedicated to the need to preserve and protect individual rights and the need to make government responsive to the needs of the majority of the people. This is a delicate balance. To achieve that balance, be moderate in all things. Our governments are suffering from a lack of moderation. The MADD mothers performed a valuable public service in reducing drunk driving but, not content with that, seek to go after the moderate drinker. The ACLU got rid of official school-sponsored prayers but now hunt the name of God with dogs. The antismokers got the smoke-free environment they sought but now seek to prevent smoking in places where they never need be. Pro-life, pro-choice, gays, the religious right, the NRA, the anti-gun lobby—there is no end to the various groups who will propose policy and spending decisions to you.

If we could offer one rule by which all these competing ideas can be judged, it would be this—the Rule of Slack, as in "cut me some slack." Ask the people who propose any policy to you how much slack they are willing to cut to those who oppose the policy. If they are unwilling to recognize the concerns of the other side, what they propose is probably an unworkable idea. If they are willing to cut some slack—to consider how others who do not think or behave as they do will react to their proposal—it is probably a workable idea.

Your duty in office is to make our government work. Winning the election is only the start. Building a consensus and winning the people to your plans and programs by making our government work is the real victory.

CONCLUSION

On that winning note, we will stop, but we feel compelled to mention, just one more time, the dictates of this book:

1. Check your local laws and regulations.
2. Plan ahead.
3. Organize.
4. Work hard.

Good luck to you in your race, and never forget that this book is only the prologue.

INTRODUCTION
TO THE APPENDIXES

These appendixes on the CD-ROM contain sample forms and worksheets to assist you in running your campaign. They are designed to help you through some of the steps in the electioneering process. Taken altogether, they provide a general outline for organizing an effective and winning campaign. Since they relate to many of the things that you will have to do at various stages in running for office, the worksheets can be used as templates in planning the campaign or as checklists for performing each step.

There will be special problems and considerations because of the requirements of your local election laws. That is why the CD-ROM contains direct web links to your state's election office and to the state code. Throughout this book we have said "check this out" over and over. Well, this is where you get to check things out.

The most effective way to use these worksheets is to study them and then see what has to be added for your race. These worksheets are only an outline, just a skeleton for you to flesh out. Review each worksheet and discuss it with the people who are helping you. See how the items fit your race, or how they are not relevant to local conditions. Talk with your staff and "old hand" about what might be added to make them better. For example, we have a sample volunteer sign-up card that lists several general things a volunteer is usually asked to do. If you have some special task for the volunteers to do, start with our form and add your own ideas to your volunteer card.

Some worksheet items ask questions, such as the nominating petition worksheet where we pose the question, "Where do I file my petitions?" The Q and A format is used because at some point during the campaign, you will have to know the answer to each one of these questions. If you use the worksheet to prepare for the campaign, you'll have the answers ready when the question comes up.

These appendixes contain sample forms, which you can look at and then use to design your own plan and forms. For example, as you sketch out your campaign plans, use our sample campaign plan, initial planning worksheet, and week-by-week campaign planning form. For the actual work of campaigning, we have a nominating-petition worksheet, a sample volunteer card, and a sample scheduling form.

None of these forms and worksheets are carved in stone. They are a good starting place, so use them to make up your own particular forms.

We have emphasized the need for planning over and over again, and we're putting this sample plan in the appendixes to give you an idea of what a campaign plan should look like. This campaign plan uses a narrative format. Instead, the candidate may use a checklist method, which is different but not inferior. Any plan is good if it includes all the necessary parts and steps. It is having a plan, not the form it takes, that counts.

The following campaign plan was prepared and used successfully in a race for clerk of a municipal court. The court district was made up of three suburban communities and, like all races, this one had specialized problems. We present this plan to you as it was originally drafted, to give you another perspective on what a good campaign plan looks like.

Every campaign, yours included, will have its own special problems, different from the ones here. When reading this plan, keep in mind that the planning factors—such as strategy, scheduling, and volunteer organization—are basically the same all over. A good campaign plan for the office you want to run for will be remarkably similar to the one that follows.

SAMPLE CAMPAIGN PLAN

BASIC CAMPAIGN STRATEGY:
CLERK OF MUNICIPAL COURT

In preparing this plan, two factors were considered as the basis for campaign strategy. The first is the low-visibility character of the race. The office is one that most people are not familiar with. They do not know what function is performed and they are unaware that this is an elected office. So they do not come prepared to vote in the race. Additionally, the physical placement of the race on the ballot is low, so the element of voter fatigue (the tendency of voters to quit before reaching the bottom of the ballot) comes into play. It is also necessary to consider that voters relate unfavorably to the judicial system in general. Courts are places people wish to ignore.

The second major factor deals with the makeup of the district. There is no cohesive pattern within the district. There are six individual communities with diverse demographic characteristics and no unifying feature. Here again, the public concept that courts and the judiciary are something to be avoided comes into play because that attitude limits the effort of people to acquire information. Voters, especially in the areas outside of Berea, probably have limited awareness of the boundaries of the Berea Municipal Court.

These factors are not necessarily negatives. They merely require that campaign strategy take them into consideration. Low visibility and voter fatigue also mean that it takes fewer votes to win. It also points to the need to identify voters who consistently resist voter fatigue. Research into voter turnout in the district communities can help to determine areas with higher concentrations of full-ticket voters. Voters who belong to unions, activist organizations, political party clubs, and so on are more likely to vote a full ticket because they will be supplied with lists of endorsed candidates.

We can adjust for the diversity and lack of unification in the district by creating a decentralized campaign. Support groups should be developed in each community and their efforts then coordinated at a campaign center. This type of organization also lends itself to more cohesive volunteer groups since they are dealing primarily with areas in which they are familiar and with people they know.

Monthly Campaign Activity Schedule

JULY

This time would be devoted primarily to basic organizational functions. Meetings should be scheduled for the last days of June and first week of July between candidate and manager to set overall strategy and essential planning. One to two evenings should be all that is necessary. This is also the time to select a person or persons to handle scheduling. At least one meeting needs to be held to discuss fund-raising: how much will be needed and how to raise it.

This is the time to get the computer operation in gear. Find compatible software and establish the programming to be used. We especially need to get going on volunteer lists and contributor lists.

Select coordinators in each community, and arrange meetings between coordinators and manager. The first of these meetings should deal with coordinator responsibilities and their suggestions for implementing the general strategy/plan. Their input should then be included in setting the actual details of the campaign plan.

The manager should also meet with the scheduler to start setting up the campaign calendar and provide the scheduler with the information necessary to begin finding activities and events for the candidate.

Depending upon the numbers of people involved, either a group meeting with the coordinators and volunteers that have already been identified should be set up; or if this is an unwieldy number, then individual meetings for coordinators and volunteers in their areas should be arranged. The general outline of activities for which volunteers will be needed should be discussed and volunteers should be given details on what will be expected. We would then be able to determine how many people would be needed, when they would be needed, and how to recruit and develop the volunteer force to get things done. Here again, getting the volunteers involved in the planning should increase the interest and enthusiasm to get others active in the campaign.

AUGUST

This month should be spent on recruiting volunteers for activities in September and October. Coordinators and early volunteers must concentrate on this aspect. The goal is to arrange meetings for volunteers in each community where the volunteers will be told what is needed, what is involved in each task, and how to accomplish it. They will be given sign-up sheets for each of the various tasks to be done and given the opportunity to choose what they would like to do.

The second part of these training sessions will depend on the number of people involved. If there are enough people, we can organize separate groups for the different tasks. If not, then the whole group will participate in discussions on how to get these jobs done—especially in getting others to help with the tasks. Volunteers for a particular task should be given specific dates when they will be expected to perform. For instance, if a volunteer offers to have a coffee, they should provide two or three dates that are convenient for them, in late September or early October, which can be given to the scheduler to confirm; someone who wants to help out with the literature drops should be asked for a specific day and areas that they would prefer to cover. Everyone will be asked to participate in planning the campaign kickoff event.

The campaign kickoff event should be scheduled and the details worked out during August. This should be part of the basic planning done by the manager and the coordinators at their meetings and the volunteers should be made a part of it at their meetings. The campaign kickoff event should have a low ticket price so that people can be encouraged to attend. Refreshments should be simple. It might be a good idea to try and get a name guest (Senator Rhodebeck perhaps: he'll be running the next year; we could ask the governor if he's going to be in the neighborhood).

SEPTEMBER

Coordinate and finalize plans for the kickoff. Follow up with volunteers who have signed up for various tasks to be done in September. Continue to recruit new volunteers. Use the campaign kickoff to help recruit. Coordinators and volunteers should publicize the activities that have been planned.

In addition to local coffees and meetings, wherever feasible there should be one event planned in each district where volunteers can get together socially. This will provide an opportunity to bring in new people and help make the campaigning work as enjoyable as possible. The local events could be get-togethers to do endorsement cards, or do mailings, or just parties to encourage and support campaign efforts. This should be arranged by the local coordinators and volunteers.

All of these events will stress certain things; but each is an opportunity to remind volunteers to get the candidate's name out, to continually try to get others involved, and to encourage small contributions to cover costs of these events. These are not fund-raisers per se but rather ways to get a commitment of actual time and money from the volunteers. These events increase the likelihood that they will spread the word. For example, since the candidate's race is at the end of the ballot, we can make the point that volunteers should ask voters to start voting at the bottom of the ballot and work their way up.

OCTOBER

The major activity in this month should be a literature drop throughout the district. It will be necessary to coordinate a large number of people in each community and arrange to get them out to cover as much area as possible. If we have been able to generate enthusiasm and interest and have developed a cohesive group, it will be much simpler to continue the same general programs that have been developed. By this time we should have a good base of volunteers to work on this large project. In addition, we may be able to combine forces with other candidates or groups to reduce the size of the area that will have to be covered.

On the Friday before the first Saturday drop, volunteers will be invited to attend a rally to get their materials for the drop. Here again, a guest would be a good idea. The purpose of the rally is to encourage people to participate in the drop and to get encouragement and support from one another. Some kind of volunteer recognition program could be developed for this event (perhaps a dinner or two for the volunteer who has contributed the most time; flowers for the oldest volunteer, etc.).

The literature drop will be the biggest effort during the latter part of October. Volunteers will have to be called and assigned areas to cover. Backups should be arranged to cover when someone fails to show up. Transportation has to be arranged when necessary or useful. Supervisors will be needed to make sure everyone has enough supplies and to check on areas where the operation is being coordinated with other candidates.

October will also be the time when the advertising blitz will take place: Ads in local newspapers, perhaps cable ads during the final week of the campaign. We should also look at school football programs for ads but that will need to be done earlier, possibly in August.

If this program is implemented, the candidate's responsibilities will be limited almost entirely to actually getting out to meet voters and to fund-raising. These are, after all, the most effective and efficient uses that can be made of a candidate's time and energy.

BUDGET

Literature piece for drop in October (50K)	$500
Targeted mail piece and postage (5K)	1,250
Fund-raising mail pieces and postage (2K)	600
Endorsement cards (2K)	350
Advertising (Print ads—$1,500/cable—$500)	2,000
Candidate expenses (tickets, meals, etc.)	1,500
Scheduler expense	850
Campaign events	500
Consulting	250
Manager	2,000
Miscellaneous	500
Total Expenses	**$10,300**

ORGANIZATION CHART

Campaign Manager

Scheduler	Coordinator Berea	Coordinator Brookpark	Coordinator Middleburg	Media

Volunteer Captain | Volunteer Captain | Volunteer Captain

Coffees

Literature Drops

Mailings

Endorsement Cards

Meetings

Phones

Campaign Events

Initial
Planning Worksheet

T hese are the things to do when you are just thinking about running and should be done well before filing your petitions. Jot down what has to be done.

1. *Personal inventory:*
   Why are you running?
   What are your qualifications for this office?
   Prepare a candidate's biography that includes education and work experience.
   What do you hope to accomplish?
   Prepare a short statement of your goals for the office.

2. *Job description:*
   What are the duties of this office?
   Look this up in the local code.

3. *Select a campaign manager:*
   Find someone whose opinion and judgment you respect.

4. *Election statistics:*
   Check the results in previous elections to see how many votes it took to win.
   Look at the results in comparable races.
   Decide on a target number that will be needed to win.
   That number is?

5. *Local election laws:*

Get a copy of the local election laws. Read them over; know them.

6. *Financial reporting requirements:*

Get a copy of the state's financial reporting requirements, including copies of the reporting forms.

Get a financial manager, and go over the requirements together.

Outline a set of books and campaign recording procedures that will contain all the data required on the reporting forms.

7. *Start a campaign calendar:*

Mark the filing deadlines on the calendar.

8. *Get a volunteer coordinator.*

9. *Work out your basic campaign theme.*

Week-by-Week Campaign Planning Form

I
n this appendix, the planning form is a chronological list of things to do based on an eighteen-week schedule. Use this form to plan your campaign, although you will have to alter it to fit the particularities of your race.

In every election, certain dates—such as the filing deadlines and election day itself—are fixed. If you begin by filling in the fixed dates, the times for doing the other things will soon appear. Remember that you put in everything that has to be done, and that you give yourself and the campaign workers enough time to do it. It is actually pretty simple, a list of things to do, and noting the date they are done.

Week Eighteen	*Date Done*
Pick the office you want to run for.	____
Talk to your family and others.	____
Review your qualifications.	____
Get petitions from board of elections.	____
Send out news release saying you are going to run.	____
Start campaign calendar.	____

Week Seventeen	*Date Done*
Talk to the old hand.	____
Select a campaign manager.	____
Select a campaign treasurer.	____

Select a volunteer coordinator. _____

Hold first campaign staff meeting. _____

Week Sixteen   Date Done

Volunteer coordinator prepares petition-signing instructions for circulators. _____

Volunteer coordinator gets petitions out to be signed. _____

Do election statistics analysis. _____

Do demographic analysis. _____

Get maps of district. _____

See what issues people are concerned about. _____

Week Fifteen   Date Done

Second staff meeting—issue analysis. _____

Talk to the old hand. _____

Rank issues in terms of importance. _____

Formulate candidate's position on each issue. _____

Select the most important issue—your issue. _____

Prepare a written statement of the candidate's position on that issue. _____

Coin a campaign slogan. _____

Choose a campaign theme. _____

Week Fourteen   Date Done

Review statistics with staff and old hand. _____

Analyze each precinct and how many votes you can expect out of it. _____

Assign each precinct a priority in terms of how well you can expect to do there. _____

Pick your target number. _____

Start looking for speaking opportunities for the candidate. _____

Week Thirteen   Date Done

Third staff meeting—initial budget planning. _____

Estimate all internal campaign expenses such as rent, telephones, postage, stationery, copies. _____

Estimate cost of the alternative campaigning methods such as radio, television, bulk mail, first-class mail. _____

Estimate cost of printing literature, signs, etc. _____

Estimate revenue sources such as how much the candidate is willing to spend. _____

Consider other revenue sources, donations, fund-raisers, PAC money. _____

(Do not try to resolve all budget questions at this time.)

Week Twelve   **Date Done**

Volunteer coordinator to report on how the petition signing is going. _____

Prepare and design the basic campaign brochure with candidate's positions and qualifications. _____

Prepare the campaign forms to be used in headquarters —volunteer card, scheduler forms, precinct volunteer packets. _____

Week Eleven   **Date Done**

Start getting the signed petitions back from the circulators. _____

Check petitions for errors, compliance with the law. _____

Write the candidate's basic speech, incorporating the campaign theme. _____

Locate a place to be the campaign headquarters. _____

Week Ten   **Date Done**

Final check of nominating petitions. _____

File your nominating petitions. _____

Open campaign checking account; open file for financial reporting requirements. _____

Send out news release on your issue. _____

Week Nine   **Date Done**

Check your opponent's nominating petitions to see if they can't be invalidated. _____

Send thank you note to everyone who signed your petition

along with a volunteer card and a ticket to your initial fund-raiser. _____

Start lining up what is needed for the campaign headquarters—telephone, desk, computer, copier, office supplies, stationery, stamps, etc. _____

Week Eight   Date Done

Open the headquarters—send out a news release. _____

Post district map and campaign calendar in headquarters, and have campaign forms ready. _____

Start computer databases, written lists of contributors, volunteers, media addresses, etc. _____

Hold your initial fund-raiser—send out news release. _____

Week Seven   Date Done

Fourth staff meeting—final budget planning. _____

News release. _____

Line up precinct volunteers. _____

Produce radio spots. _____

Coffee—fund-raiser. _____

Week Six   Date Done

Weekly staff meeting. _____

News release. _____

Start addressing—get packets out. _____

Find precinct volunteers for remaining precincts. _____

Refine mailing list—cull names. _____

Week Five   Date Done

Weekly staff meeting. _____

News release. _____

Go door to door. _____

Addressing party at headquarters. _____

Schedule coffee. _____

Second fund-raiser. _____

Prepare draft of finance report; check for accuracy. _____

Prepare newspaper ads. _____

Week Four   *Date Done*

    Weekly staff meeting.   _____

    News release.   _____

    Go door to door.   _____

    Start radio—two spots per day.   _____

    Attend annual Party dinner.   _____

    Schedule coffee.   _____

    Check on how addressing packets is coming; push the vol-
        unteers to get them back.   _____

Week Three   *Date Done*

    Weekly staff meeting.   _____

    News release.   _____

    Go door to door.   _____

    Radio spots—three spots per day.   _____

    Start getting addressed envelopes back; final call.   _____

    Meet the Candidates Night.   _____

    Start sorting and bundling mail.   _____

    File preelection finance report.   _____

    Candidate rest day.   _____

Week Two   *Date Done*

    Weekly staff meeting.   _____

    News release.   _____

    Go door to door.   _____

    Start newspaper ads.   _____

    Radio—five spots per day.   _____

    Finish bundling—mail first part of mailing.   _____

    Check on absentee ballots.   _____

    Schedule coffee.   _____

Week One   *Date Done*

    Weekly staff meeting.   _____

    News release.   _____

    Go door to door.   _____

    Radio spots—five per day.   _____

Do second half of bulk mailing. _____
Schedule coffee. _____

Day One   Date Done

Schedule poll workers. _____
Schedule drivers. _____
Hold victory party. _____
Start preparing postcampaign financial report. _____

When you write it all out like this, it seems like a lot, but you will probably do almost every item on this list and more. Use a plan like this to keep yourself from being overwhelmed. Put them in one at a time, do them one at a time, and check them off one at a time.

NOMINATING-PETITION WORKSHEET

Y ou have to get the petitions out, signed, back, checked, and properly filed. Begin by reading the requirements for the petitions and the signatures in the election law handbook. You should know the answer to every question posed below.

1. *How many signatures?*

    The minimum number of signatures required is: _____.

    The maximum number of signatures allowed is: _____.

    Is there a limit on the number of petitions that may be filed?

2. *Petition circulators*

    What are the qualifications by law for a person who circulates petitions? _____

    The circulators names are: _____

    _____

    _____

3. *Valid signatures*

    A valid signature usually must contain the name, address, and voting residence of the signer, who must be a registered voter.

    What other requirements are there?

    Party affiliation _____

Voting district _____

Will your circulator need that information? _____

4. *How are petitions validated?*

Does the circulator sign the petition? _____

Do you need to notarize the petition? _____

Will errors (erasures or a signature by someone not registered) invalidate the entire petition? _____

Must all signers on any one petition be from the same voting district? _____

5. *Where are petitions filed?* _____

6. *When must they be filed?* _____

7. *Which member of the campaign will check each petition for
accuracy and compliance before it is filed?* _____
_____

8. *When is the filing date?* _____

9. *The person in charge of filing the petitions on time is:* _____
_____.

Sample Volunteer Card

W e use the term "volunteer card" because a printed 3 x 5 index card is the handiest format, but these can be done on a sheet of paper. The most important thing is to have them ready at all times and to have the form contain a space for any kind of activity you might think you will need volunteers for during the campaign.

SAMPLE VOLUNTEER CARD

CITIZENS FOR _____
I want to help elect _____ to City Council.
Name _____
Address _____
                                                  (zip code)
Phone: Home_____ Cell _____
I can help by making a contribution of _____
I cannot contribute, but I can help by:

_____making phone calls
_____sponsoring a coffee/brunch
_____putting up a yard sign
_____typing, mailing, addressing envelopes
_____computers
_____distributing literature
_____driving, giving rides
_____registering voters
_____have candidate speak to my group
_____other: _____

APPENDIX F

SAMPLE SCHEDULING FORM

The scheduler will use this form to schedule all candidate appearances. Be sure the volunteers get a copy because many of them will know of an event where the candidate can appear.

SCHEDULING FORM

All potential events where the candidate might appear must be scheduled, to make sure he gets there on time and to avoid conflicts. Anyone who knows of an event should fill out this scheduling form. Tell us about it. It might only be a small group, but if there is nothing scheduled at that time the candidate can show up. We're going to win this a few votes at a time.

There might be a better opportunity elsewhere and we will have to decide which event the candidate should attend, but the scheduler has to know about all possible events. Fill in all the information below, so we can set our priorities. Thanks!

1. Event _____

                  (what kind of event)

2. Day _____ 3. Time _____

4. Place _____

---

5. Number Expected _____

6. Candidate's Opportunity _____

_____

(speaking, meeting people, media coverage, interview, etc.)

7. Contact _____   _____

             (person sponsoring event)   (phone)

8. Special Instructions _____

9. Your name and phone _____

DIRECTORY OF STATE ELECTIONS OFFICERS

The following is a list of the chief elections directors for each state in alphabetical order. You can obtain a copy of your state's election laws and campaign financial reporting requirements by writing to the state elections director. This information is often also available at your local elections office. You should obtain this information and read it over before beginning any political campaign.

These offices also maintain voters' lists and usually make that information available either in hard copy or on computer tapes or disks at a reasonable cost. In some states, voter lists are available locally. A good voter list is absolutely necessary to any campaign, and getting a computerized list is the best option. (See Chapter 9 for more on using computers in your campaign.)

Alabama
Administrator of Elections
State House, Rm. 21
Montgomery, AL 36130

Director of Voter Registration
State House, Rm. 129
Montgomery,
AL 36130

Alaska
Director of Elections
P.O. Box AF
Juneau, AK 99811-0105

Arizona
State Election Officer
1700 W. Washington
Phoenix, AZ 85007

Arkansas
Supervisor of Elections
State Capitol, Rm. 206
Little Rock, AR 72201

California
Chief, Elections and Political
Reform
1230 J Street
Sacramento, CA 95814

Colorado
Elections Officer
Department of State
1560 Broadway, Ste. 200
Denver, CO 80202

Connecticut
Manager, Elections Services
30 Trinity Street
Hartford, CT 06106

Delaware
State Election Commissioner
32 Loockerman Square, Ste. 203
Dover, DE 19901

District of Columbia
Executive Director
Board of Elections and Ethics
350 Pennsylvania Avenue NW
Washington, DC 20004

Florida
Director, Division of Elections
The Capitol, Rm. 1801
Tallahassee,
FL 32399-0250

Georgia
Director, Elections Division
State Capitol, Rm. 110
Atlanta, GA 30334

Hawaii
Director of Elections
Office of Lt. Governor
State Capitol, 5th Fl.
Honolulu, HI 96813

Idaho
Chief Deputy Secretary of
State for Elections
203 State House
Boise, ID 83720

Illinois
Executive Director
State Board of Elections
1020 S. Spring Street
P.O. Box 4187
Springfield, IL 62708

Assistant to the Executive
Director
State Board of Elections
State of Illinois Center
100 W. Randolph, Ste. 14-100
Chicago, IL 60601

Indiana
Executive Director
State Board of Elections
302 W. Washington, Rm. C032
Indianapolis,
IN 46204

Iowa
Director of Elections
Office of the Secretary of State
Hoover Building, 2nd Fl.
Des Moines, IA 50319

Kansas
Deputy Assistant for Elections
and Legislative Matters
Capitol Building
Topeka, KS 66612

Kentucky
Executive Director
State Board of Elections
State Capitol, Rm. 71
Frankfort, KY 40601

Louisiana
Administrator, Election
Division
State Capitol, 19th Fl.
P.O. Box 94215
Baton Rouge, LA 70804-9125

Executive Officer, Department
of Elections and Registration
P.O. Box 14179
Baton Rouge, LA 70898-4179

Maine
Director of Elections
State House Ste. 101
Augusta, ME 04333

Maryland
Deputy Administrator, State
Admissions Board of Election
P.O. Box 231
Annapolis, MD 21404-0231

Massachusetts
Director of Elections
Election Division, Rm. 1705
One Ashburton Place
Boston, MA 02108

Michigan
Director of Elections
Department of State
Mutual Building, 4th Fl.
208 N. Capitol Avenue
Lansing, MI 48918

Minnesota
Director, Election Division
180 State Office Building
St. Paul, MN 55155

Mississippi
Assistant Secretary of State
P.O. Box 136
Jackson, MS 39025

Missouri
Deputy Secretary of State for
Election Services
Truman Office Building, Rm.
780, Jefferson City, MO 65102

Montana
Election Bureau Chief, Office
of the Secretary of State
State Capitol, Rm. 225
Helena, MT 59620

Nebraska
Deputy Secretary of State and
Director of Elections
State Capitol, Ste. 2300
Lincoln, NE 68509

Nevada
Deputy Secretary of State for
Elections
Capitol Complex
Carson City, NV 89710

Chief Deputy Secretary of
State
Office of the Secretary of State
Capitol Complex
Carson City, NV 89710

New Hampshire
Secretary of State
State House, Rm. 204
Concord, NH 03301

New Jersey
Director, Election Division
Department of State
Trenton, NJ 08625-0304

New Mexico
Director, Bureau of Elections
State Capitol Building, 4th Fl.
Santa Fe, NM 87503

New York
Executive Director
State Board of Elections
Swan Street Building, Core 1
Empire State Plaza
Albany, NY 12260

North Carolina
Executive Secretary/Director
State Board of Elections
P.O. Box 1166
Raleigh, NC 27602

North Dakota
Secretary of State
State Capitol, 1st Fl.
Bismarck, ND 68509

Ohio
Elections Administrator
Office of the Secretary of State
30 East Broad Street, 14th Fl.
Columbus, OH 43266-0418

Oklahoma
Secretary, State Election Board
3-B State Capitol Building
Oklahoma City, OK 73152

Oregon
Director of Elections
Office of the Secretary of State
141 State Capitol
Salem, OR 97310

Pennsylvania
Commissioner of Elections
305 North Office Building
Harrisburg, PA 17120

Puerto Rico
President
State Election Commission
Old San Juan Sta., P.O. Box
2353
San Juan, PR 00902-2353

Rhode Island
Chairman
State Board of Elections
50 Branch Street
Providence, RI 09204

South Carolina
Executive Director
State Election Commission
P.O. Box 5987
Columbia, SC 29250

South Dakota
Supervisor of Elections
500 E. Capitol
Pierre, SD 57501-5077

Tennessee
Coordinator of Elections
James K. Polk Building, Ste. 500
Nashville, TN 37219

Texas
Special Assistant for Elections
P.O. Box 12060
Austin, TX 78711

Utah
Lt. Governor's Office
State Capitol Building, Rm. 203
Salt Lake City, UT 84114

Vermont
Director of Elections
Office of the Secretary of State
Montpelier, VT 05602-2198

Virgin Islands
Supervisor of Elections
V.I. Board of Elections
P.O. Box 6038
St. Thomas, VI 00801

Virginia
Secretary
State Board of Elections
Ninth Street Office Bldg., Rm. 101
Richmond, VA 23219

Washington
Election Director
Office of the Secretary of State
Olympia, WA 98504

West Virginia
Deputy Secretary of State
State Capitol, Rm. 157-K
Charleston, WV 25305

Wisconsin
Executive Director
State Elections Board
132 East Wilson Street, 3rd Fl.
Madison, WI 53702

Wyoming
Deputy Secretary of State
Capitol Building, Rm. 106
Cheyenne, WY 82002-0020

GLOSSARY OF TERMS

Absentee ballot. If a voter is disabled, over a certain age, or will be out of town on election day, he may obtain an absentee ballot ahead of time. The vote is sealed and counted on election day.

At large. An at-large race is in the entire political subdivision, instead of smaller districts. For example, a mayor would run at large in the city, but a councilman would run from a single ward.

Board of elections. The agency that conducts elections and administers the election laws, sometimes including financial and ethics reporting requirements.

Campaign. A race for elective office and the steps taken to ensure victory.

Campaign calendar. A large wall-mounted calendar used in campaign headquarters to schedule all events.

Campaign manager; campaign chairman. The person in charge of the overall campaign planning and coordination.

Campaign plan. A plan, drafted early in the campaign, detailing each step needed to win the election.

Campaign theme. A statement of a principle, an idea, or phrase that summarizes and captures the spirit of the campaign.

Census district. A geographical block or area, such as a city block, by which the Census Bureau gathers data; census-district data is a good source of local demographic information, available at most libraries.

Contribution. A donation to a campaign. Under many state laws, the donation of property or even the loan of property must be reported as a contribution.

Crossover voting. Where people from one party vote in a primary election for candidates of the other party. *See also* Open primary.

District. As used in this book, the geographical boundaries of the office for which you are running (e.g., township, ward).

Elections director. The person in charge of the state's elections laws. *See also* State elections director.

Elections office. The board of elections or local office that manages the electoral process.

Election statistics. Past election results broken down by various criteria, such as by voters' political party or geographic region. They are analyzed in the planning stage to calculate how many votes it will take to win in the present.

Elector. A person registered and eligible to vote.

Ethics report. *See* Financial report.

Ethnic voter. A voter who identifies himself with a certain class, racial or religious group, or subculture; often used for nationalities but broadly applied to any group.

Expenditure. Any use of funds that is required by the laws of your state to be reported on the financial reporting form.

Filing deadline. The date on which a petition, finance report, or other document is required by the state's election law to be filed.

Filing petitions. *See* Nominating petitions.

Finance chairman. The campaign volunteer who is in charge of maintaining records of all income and expenditures and is responsible for filing all financial reports.

Financial report. A statement of income and expenses that is required by law to be reported. It may be required of the candidate, the campaign committee, or both. Many states require at least two filings, one before the election and one after.

General election. The election held to decide who will hold that office. The general election is usually held in November. *See also* Primary election.

High-profile race. An election contest that voters are interested in and want to hear about. *See also* Low-profile race.

Independent candidate. A candidate who is not nominated by a party. One who runs in the general election.

Independent voter. A voter who does not identify with a political party and may not vote in primary elections.

Low-profile race. A race that does not generate much public interest or where the voters are not much concerned about the office (e.g., coroner). *See also* High-profile race.

Name; ballot name. The name of the candidate as it appears on the ballot. Check your local laws about nicknames, maiden names, legal name changes, and the like.

Name game. Where the candidate relies on a popular, well-known name as part of his strategy.

Name identification. The recognition of the candidate's name and association of the name with an idea by the voter.

Nominating petitions. In order to get on the ballot, a candidate must obtain the signatures of a certain number of registered voters on a petition. These petitions are obtained at the elections office. Strict compliance with the regulations is required for all nominating petitions.

Nonpartisan. Not related to any party. In nonpartisan elections, the candidate's party affiliation does not appear on the ballot.

Off-year election. An election, usually local, held in a year when there are no high-profile elections such as those for governor, senator, or president.

Old hand. A person with a lot of experience in elections; one who knows the ropes.

Open primary. A primary election to nominate the party's candidates for the general election where members of the other party and Independents are permitted to vote. *See also* Crossover voting.

Partisan. Relating to a political party. In partisan elections the candidate's party affiliation appears on the ballot.

Part petition. A single-sheet nominating petition that is combined with other part petitions to make up the nominating petition.

Political action committee (PAC). A political special interest group, particularly one whose function is to collect money from its members to contribute to sympathetic candidates.

Political committee. Generally speaking, a committee organized to achieve some political result. Each state has laws defining political committees and regulating their activities. Always check your local laws on this.

Political map. A map of the electoral district with the lines for each electoral precinct drawn in.

Polling place. The place where people vote.

Precinct. The smallest electoral area. Each precinct generally has one polling place.

Precinct by precinct. The winning strategy of having a worker in each precinct and getting a targeted number of votes out of each precinct.

Precinct committeeman or committeewoman. The party member who represents his or her precinct in party affairs; often the volunteer in the precinct-by-precinct strategy.

Precinct map. A map of the precinct, used to assist in the precinct-by-precinct strategy.

Primary election. An election to select the party's nominees for the general election, usually held in the spring but always some time before the general election. *See also* General election.

Registered voter. A person listed on the books of the elections office as being eligible to vote.

Scheduler. Campaign volunteer charged with maintaining the campaign calendar and scheduling all events.

Scheduling form. The form used by the scheduler to organize the scheduling. See Appendix F for a sample.

Special election. An election held not at the regularly scheduled time, usually for one special purpose (e.g., a tax levy or to fill a vacancy in office).

State elections director. The chief operations officer of the state's electoral system, usually the one charged with providing information about the regulations, laws, and requirements for candidates. Often the judge in election disputes.

Swing voters and swing precincts. A term used in analyzing election statistics to describe persons and areas where the voters are not tied to either party but can be reached by an effective campaign.

Target number. The winning number; the specific number of votes the candidate estimates is necessary to win in that area. The number of votes the candidate will try to get in that area.

Three-way race. A race with more than two candidates, usually one with a Republican, a Democrat, and an Independent. Sometimes it is used to designate a race where all candidates run at large and the top three vote getters are elected.

Volunteer. A campaign worker; one who helps out doing the many things that have to be done in any campaign.

Volunteer card. Form used to organize campaign volunteers and to schedule their duties. See Appendix E for a sample.

Volunteer coordinator. Campaign volunteer in charge of all other volunteers and who coordinates their efforts.

Voter fatigue. The tendency of voters, even the ones who go to the polls, not to vote in every race on the ballot. Voter fatigue is greatest in low-profile races.

Voter list. A list of all persons registered to vote in an area. Voter lists are usually maintained by precinct and are public records available to candidates for electioneering purposes.

INDEX